monday morning®

Book Boosters

by Murray Suid

Illustrated by Marilynn G. Barr

This book is for Marcella Suid

Publisher: Roberta Suid
Design: David Hale
Copy Editor: Carol Whiteley
Typesetting: Santa Monica Press
Production: Susan Pinkerton
Consultants: Sue Krumbein, Wanda Lincoln

Monday Morning books related to this topic are: *How to Create Picture Books* (MM1983), *Storybooks Teach Writing* (MM1990), *Ten-Minute Whole Language Warm-ups* (MM1955), *Picture Book Factory* (MM1933)

CONTENTS

INTRODUCTION

Book Boosters introduces students to a wide variety of language arts projects based on real-world models. Formats include: letters, scripts, diaries, maps, time lines, sequels, museum displays, panels, interviews, murals, and TV shows. The book aims to help language artists:
- appreciate, analyze, and share literature
- sharpen writing, performing, and art skills
- master subject matter throughout the curriculum

This approach is called "whole learning."

HOW TO USE THE BOOK

Book Boosters is organized alphabetically. There is no one right place to begin. Think of this guide as a cookbook, and select projects that meet your students' needs.

The index may come in handy. For example, if you want to focus on vocabulary development, you'll find word-oriented projects in the index. If you're planning a unit on TV production, the index lists video activities.

The lessons all share a similar structure:
- **Directions.** Each activity is built around a step-by step sequence. The directions can be read aloud to students or reproduced as handouts.
- **Models.** A story or other sample is included to clarify each assignment. For the sake of familiarity, the models often deal with picture books, fables, or fairy tales. Of course, the activities are designed to be done with books at every level. For example, the vocabulary-building project "Book-tionary" would work as well with the novel *Tuck Everlasting* as it does with the picture book *There's Something in My Attic.*
- **Follow-up.** An extension activity reinforces each lesson by applying the key skill to another situation. For example, after writing a fictional letter to the editor from a character's viewpoint, students use the same form to write a real letter to a hometown newspaper.

WHAT KIND OF LITERATURE SHOULD YOU "BOOST?"

Students need to read not only lots of books, but lots of different kinds of books. While some of the activities focus on either fiction or nonfiction, many of the projects work with both. For example, "Letter to a Reading Pal" is equally challenging if a reader is recommending *Julia of the Wolves* (a novel) or *Daring the Unknown* (a history of NASA).

Projects often cut across subject matter boundaries. For example, a book review dealing with an explorer's autobiography can involve weather (science), keeping a diary (language arts), and math (average speed).

SPECIAL RESOURCES

At the end of the book, you'll find tips for using video and other media, encouraging self-evaluation, and carrying out whole-class projects.

You'll also find an extensive list of the best guides to children's literature. These widely available reference books cover all types of literature for students reading at many levels.

WHAT'S WHOLE LEARNING? LOOK IN A MIRROR!

Whole learning is not complex. Think about how you learn yourself: by reading books, watching TV, chatting with friends, attending conferences, and so on. Think about how you reinforce your knowledge: by sharing it through letter writing, putting up bulletin boards, participating in meetings, acting as a model, and so on.

The point is: *You* are a whole learner. As such, you're the best resource for creating a whole learning environment for your students. Trust your instincts and your students will succeed.

Action Map

Each place in a story is called a "setting." A story might have many settings. For example, the settings in *Cinderella* include Cinderella's house, the pumpkin coach, and the castle's ballroom.

Directions:
1. In a book that you have read, choose an important setting where one or a few actions happen.
2. Draw a map or bird's-eye-view diagram of the place. Label each important part, for example, "playground."
3. On the map, add pictures, symbols, or words that point out each action.
4. Give the map a title that includes the name of the book and the author's name. Write a short introduction that explains why the setting is important to the story.

Follow-up:
Find a fiction or nonfiction book that is set in one or more real places. For example, *Make Way for Ducklings* takes place in Boston. Use an atlas or other reference to draw a map of where some or all of the action happens. On the map, use labels to point out the action or actions.

SAMPLE ACTION MAP

Mapping *Ira Sleeps Over*
by Bernard Waber

Ira is a kid who's going to spend the night at Reggie's house next door. Ira is excited because it's his first sleep-over. But he doesn't know if he should take his teddy bear with him. He doesn't like to sleep without his teddy, but he doesn't want to look like a baby.

During the story, Ira goes back and forth from his house to his friend's house. The fact that the two houses are close together makes it possible for Ira to make one important last trip even though it's late at night.

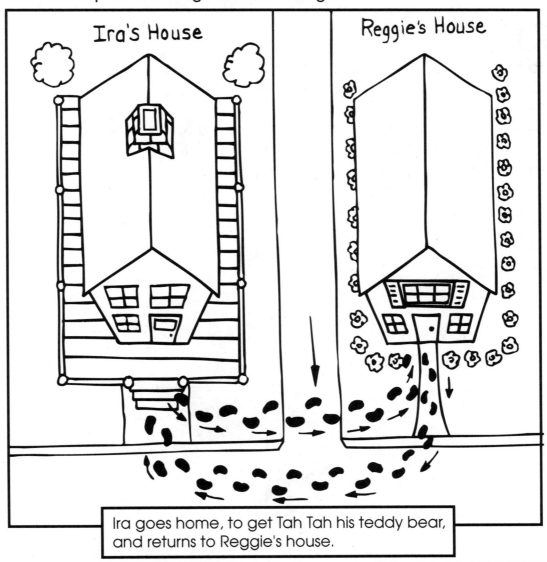

Ira goes home, to get Tah Tah his teddy bear, and returns to Reggie's house.

Adapt a Book

Many books are turned into movies, plays, or other creative forms. Doing this kind of translation is called "making an adaptation."

Directions:
1. Choose a book to adapt. It could be fiction or nonfiction. If you've never made an adaptation before, it's best to work with a short book.
2. Decide what form you'll turn the book into. The following types are often used:
   - movies
   - plays
   - puppet shows
   - television programs
3. Read the book carefully, and list the ideas or actions you want to include. You might decide to adapt only part of the book. Or you could cover the whole story by leaving out details.
4. Write a script. Keep it simple. Hint: Having a narrator talk to the audience is one way to simplify a story. The narrator can sum up in a few words what might take several scenes to present through actions.
5. Read the script aloud and make changes that are needed. This could include adding or cutting lines. The title of the final script should include the title of the book and the author's name.

Follow-up:
Use the script you wrote to put on a puppet play, a TV program, or other type of show.

SAMPLE ADAPTATION

The Ant and the Grasshopper: A Puppet Script Based on a Story by Aesop

Narrator: One summer day, a grasshopper hops over a hedge and lands near an anthill.

Grasshopper: Wheeeeeeee!

Narrator: The grasshopper watches a busy ant drag a piece of food to the opening of the anthill.

Grasshopper: Hello, ant. What's going on?

Ant: (huffing and puffing) I can't talk now. There's so much work to be done before winter. If I'm going to eat this winter, I have to work now.

Grasshopper: But it's only July.

Ant: I'll be lucky if I'm done by November.

Grasshopper: Well, you won't catch me working so hard. Not in this wonderful weather. (The grasshopper lies down and begins to snore.)

Narrator: The days and weeks go by, and the ant continues to work. The weather changes. Then one day in December, snow begins to fall.

Grasshopper: (stirs from sleep) Hey, it's cold. And I'm hungry. (looks around) But I don't see any food. (goes to anthill) Hey, ant, are you down there? Can you give me some food?

Ant: (calling from offstage) You should have worked instead of sleeping.

Grasshopper: The ant is right. But I wish I had learned that lesson a little earlier.

The End

Advertise a Book

"Advertise" comes from a Latin word that means "to turn toward." An advertising writer tries to turn the audience toward a product, so that they'll want to buy or use it. The product might be anything, even a book.

Directions:
1. Choose a favorite book of yours that other readers might enjoy. It can be fiction or nonfiction.
2. List things you like about the book, for example:
   - a smart hero
   - interesting places or facts
   - an exciting ending
3. Write a newspaper or magazine advertisement that sells the book. This kind of advertisement often includes the following parts:
   - a headline of seven or fewer words
   - a description of the book, including its title and author
   - information about the kind of reader who might like the book
   - a list of the book's good points (called "selling points")
   - a picture of the book or a scene from the book
4. Include the finished advertisement in a classroom newspaper, or turn it into a poster for a bulletin board.

Follow-up:
Create an advertisement for a film or television show.

SAMPLE BOOK ADVERTISEMENT

Play Ball!

Do you love baseball? Would you like to improve your skills? Then you should read *Hitting, Pitching, and Fielding* by Hal Higdon.

This 127-page book is filled with hints from famous major league players, including Dusty Baker, Johnny Bench, Bobby Bonds, Steve Garvey, and Mike Hargrove.

Six chapters cover hitting, pitching, catching, running, the infield, and the outfield.

The book is special because it includes:
- many action photographs
- words spoken by famous players
- suggestions for beginning and advanced players
- information about equipment

This book may not make you into a superstar, but it can help you play better than you thought you could.

Advice for a Character

In most books, the heroes face difficult problems. How lucky they'd be if they could get help from readers.

Directions:
1. Find a book with a character who has lots of problems or one big problem. For example, the character might be bored with school or might be afraid of a bully.
2. Figure out what the character should do to solve the problem or problems.
3. Write the character a letter, and explain your plan for what the character should do. Give your paper a title or introduction that includes the title of the story and the author's name.

Follow-up:
Write an advice letter to a real person. It can be someone you know, or it can be someone famous, like your town's mayor.

SAMPLE ADVICE LETTER

A Letter to Humpty Dumpty, the Hero of
Humpty Dumpty **by Mother Goose**

August 18

Dear Humpty,

The last time I was in town, I saw you sitting on a high wall. This is a very dangerous thing to do. Because of your rounded shape, you can easily roll. If this happens while you are on the top of a wall, you might go over the edge and have a great fall.

Maybe you never looked down from the wall, but at the bottom is a concrete sidewalk. Do you know what might happen to you if you hit that concrete after falling off the wall? It would be a big mess.

I know what you're thinking. You are friends with the king, so you think his royal highness would send all his men and horses to patch you up. This is a bad idea. I'm sure the king would send the horses and men, but I doubt that they could put you together again.

For this reason, I hope you will listen to me and not sit on the wall. But if for some reason you have to sit up there, please put a pillow near the bottom of the wall. This way, in case you do fall, you might not break into dozens of pieces.

Sincerely,

A. Reader

Be a Barker

Step right up! Here's a chance to run off to the circus without leaving school. Just as a circus barker invites people to enter the tent to see the show, a reader can urge other readers to "enter" a good book. This kind of presentation is called a "pitch" or a "spiel."

Directions:
1. While reading your book, make a list of unusual or exciting happenings that occur in it. For example, in the storybook *Time to get out of the bath, Shirley*, a little girl named Shirley:
- goes down the bathtub drain;
- meets a knight in shining armor;
- visits a castle; and
- playfully knocks a king into a lake.

2. Write a sales pitch that tells about some of the fascinating sights to be seen inside your book. Be sure to include the name of the book and the author. Most barkers try to hook the audience with the sentence: "Step right up!" But you might invent your own "hook."

3. Rehearse your spiel before giving it to an audience. Talk in a big, loud voice. Use large hand gestures. Let people know how excited you are about what's inside the book.

4. When you give your presentation, you might wear a straw hat and wave a stick the way barkers do when they pitch a show at the circus.

Follow-up:
Create a spiel for a story that you have written. Or give a pitch for an activity such as using a microscope or working on the classroom newspaper.

SAMPLE BARKER SPIEL

Spiel for *James and the Giant Peach*

Step right up! Yes, come on in! Enter the amazing world of Roald Dahl's *James and the Giant Peach*.

You'll see a peach as large as a car, a talking centipede, and a talking spider. You'll go on a tumbling ride down a hill inside a peach. No roller coaster in the world is as exciting. That's just the beginning. Then you'll take an ocean voyage to faraway lands. You'll meet weird creatures. You'll have close calls.

And in the end . . . Well, to find out, you'll have to come on in. Do it now. The only expense is your time.

Bibliography

A bibliography is a list of books on a topic. This kind of list is often found at the end of a nonfiction book. It tells where some of the information came from. It can also help readers decide what to read next if they want to learn more about the topic.

Directions:
1. Choose a book that doesn't have a bibliography. It could be nonfiction or fiction.
2. Go to the library and find at least two books on the book's main topic.
3. List the books in alphabetical order. For each one, include:
- the title
- the author
- the publisher
- the date the book was published
- a few sentences that describe the book

4. Label this list of books "Bibliography for _____" and fill in the name of the book and the author, for example, "Bibliography for *A Wrinkle in Time* by Madeleine L'Engle." Include a short introduction that explains what the bibliography has to do with the book.

Follow-up:
Create a bibliography for the next report you write, or for a book that you might like to write some day.

SAMPLE BIBLIOGRAPHY

Bibliography for *Goldilocks and the Three Bears* retold by James Marshall

Goldilocks had no business going into the three bears' cottage. Even though she was very curious, she should have stayed outside. It seems to me that she could use a few lessons about manners. The following books might be helpful to her.

The Muppet Guide to Magnificent Manners by James Howe (Random House, 1984). This book gives readers advice about introductions, conversations, telephone calls, table manners, parties, visits, and letter writing. It has a funny introduction by Miss Piggy. There are also many silly pictures showing Sesame Street characters.

Perfect Pigs by Marc Brown and Stephen Krensky (Little, Brown, 1983). This book of manners shows how to behave around the house, with your family, during meals, with pets, at parties, at school, during games, and in public places. It's written like a comic book, and gives lots of helpful hints, for example, "Don't keep friends waiting" and "Don't make fun of other people."

What Should You Say, Dear? by Joy Berry (Children's Press, 1983). This book is all about getting along with other people. It tells the right way to introduce yourself to someone you don't know, and how to introduce people you know to each other. There are examples of how to solve problems, for example, if you forget a person's name. It also shows how to begin and end a conversation in a way that seems very grown up. One of the most useful parts is about giving apologies, for example, if you break something that belongs to someone else.

Book Bag Report

Like Santa's sack, a good book contains all sorts of terrific surprises. Sharing some of them is a fun way to interest potential readers.

Directions:
1. As you read your book, make a list of interesting objects that are important to the story. For example, in *Cinderella*, the list might include the mirror and the poisoned apple.
2. Choose four or five of the objects. Then draw a picture of each one or find a real example. For instance, if one of the things on your list is a key, you might use a real key.
3. Write a short introduction that gives the book's title and author. The introduction should also explain what the book is about.
4. Write a few sentences about each object.
5. Put all the drawings and real things into a bag.
6. Rehearse your presentation. As you talk, bring out the pictures and things one at a time. Use them to tell about your book.
7. Give your presentation for real.

Follow-up:
Do the same activity when giving a speech about a real experience that happened to you. For example, you might do a "bag" report about your summer vacation or about how to play a game like chess.

SAMPLE BOOK BAG REPORT

Bag of Things to Present
The Wonderful Wizard of Oz

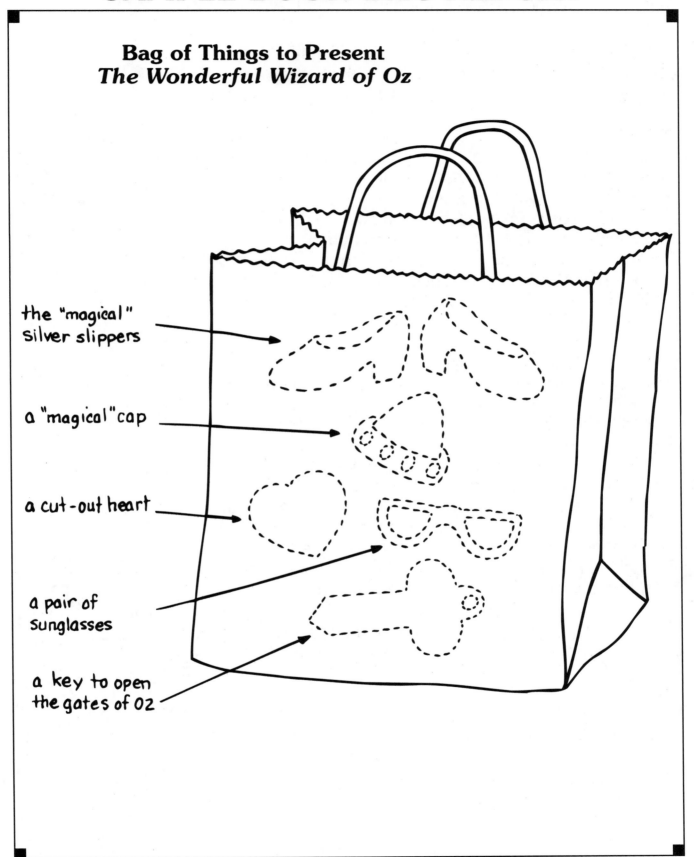

the "magical" silver slippers

a "magical" cap

a cut-out heart

a pair of sunglasses

a key to open the gates of OZ

Book Jacket

A book jacket does two important jobs. First, it keeps a book clean and dry. Second, it gives information about the book's content and the book's author.

Directions:

1. Find a book that doesn't have a book jacket. You might get one at home, or ask your librarian if he or she has one that you can work with.
2. Read the book. Take notes on the book's content.
3. Gather information about the book's author:
   - year of birth and, if dead, year of death
   - birthplace and other places lived
   - education and work experience
   - family
   - other books written
   - hobbies and interests

Most libraries have reference books that contain the facts you need. You can also write to the book's publisher.

4. Draft the words for the jacket:
   - On the front cover put the book's title, the author's name, and the illustrator's name (if there is one).
   - On the inside front flap describe the book's content. Continue on the inside back flap if space is needed.
   - On the inside back flap give facts about the author.
   - On the back cover make a list of the contents or include quotations from readers who like the book.
5. Add art on the front of the jacket. It should give a hint of the book's content.
6. After copying the material onto a clean piece of paper, laminate it or cover it with plastic wrap.
7. Attach the jacket to the book.

Follow-up:

Create a book jacket for a book that you might like to write some day.

SAMPLE BOOK JACKET

Book Jacket for
Alice's Adventures in Wonderland

Books on Tape

These days many busy people "read" by listening to tape-recorded books. Sometimes the voice belongs to the book's author. But often it's a professional reader, someone who is good at reading aloud.

Directions:
1. Choose a book that you would like to share with a friend, a relative, a pen pal, or even a stranger.
2. Decide how much of the book you want to tape record. If it's a short children's book, you might record the whole thing. If it's a long book, you might choose a sample chapter.
3. Write a short introduction that tells the listener the title of the book, what the book is about, the name of the author, and the name of the reader—you. The introduction should also tell how much of the book you plan to read.
4. Rehearse the material you plan to record before recording it.
5. When you're done recording, write the title of the book, your name, and the date on the cassette.
6. Give the tape to someone who will listen to it.

Follow-up:
Tape record a story that you have written. Share the tape with someone who will enjoy listening to you read your work. You might send the tape to a friend or relative living in another city.

BOOKS-ON-TAPE STUDIO

Book-tionary

There's more to a book than its plot or contents. Every book is like a can of words, a meal that can build strong vocabularies fast.

Directions:

1. As you read your book, choose five words that you never read before. Or choose words that you have seen but want to understand better.
2. For each word, try to find the following in a dictionary:
   - the word's origin (where it came from)
   - the word's pronunciation (how you say it)
   - other words that relate to the word (for example, "moon" and "month" are related)

In addition to using the dictionary, you could talk with someone who knows about the subject. For example, if "moon" is one of your words, an astronomer could give you useful information.

3. Write an essay about your words. The introduction should tell the title of the book and what the book is about. Then list the words and the information that you found.

Follow-up:

Do the same activity, but instead of taking words from a book, take them from your own life. For example, if you are interested in quicksand, that might be one of your words.

SAMPLE BOOK-TIONARY

Words from *There's Something in My Attic* by Mercer Mayer

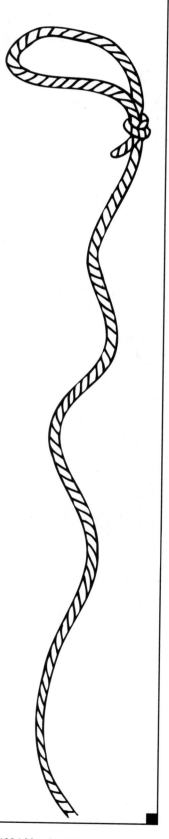

Most people have had nightmares. *There's Something in My Attic* shows what to do if a nightmare comes to you. It says you should bravely face your fears.

The story is told by a girl whose family has moved from the city to a big house in the country. In this new house, there are strange sounds. The heroine thinks she hears a nightmare in the attic, and decides to capture it with a lasso.

The girl catches the nightmare and drags it downstairs toward her parents' bedroom. She wakes her parents, but the thing disappears. The little girl thinks that maybe she'll be able to outsmart the nightmare the next time she hears it.

Here are five interesting words found in the book.

Amaze means to surprise or confuse. It relates to the word "maze," which is a set of winding paths in which people can get lost.

Attic is a room or space just below the roof of a house. It usually has a sloping ceiling. The word comes from the French word "attique."

Lasso is a rope with a sliding loop, used by cowboys and cowgirls to catch cattle and wild horses. The word comes from the Spanish word "lazo."

Nightmare is a scary dream. The word "mare" can mean "female horse" but it has another meaning, which is "evil spirit." Long ago, people thought that evil spirits caused bad dreams.

Teddy bear is a stuffed toy bear. It was named for Teddy Roosevelt, the twenty-sixth president of the United States.

Box a Book

Soap, cereal, and cake mixes are just a few things that come in boxes. But what if books were packaged that way?

Directions:

1. Study a few boxes that contain different kinds of products. Notice the different things that appear on the box. These usually include:
   - product name
   - what the product is made of (ingredients)
   - steps for using the product
   - words telling why the product is special ("new," "easy to use," and so on)
   - name of the company that made the product
   - picture of the product

2. Find a box that you can use to present information about a book you have read. Cover the box with blank paper.

3. Put different kinds of information on each side (called a "panel") of the box. For example, on the front panel you might draw a picture of the book, including its title and author. On the back panel you might show scenes from the book. The sides could give reasons for reading the book.

4. Find a place to show off the box, for example, in a classroom or a library.

Follow-up:

Make a box autobiography of your life. One side might give your birth date and other facts, other sides might describe hobbies or skills that you are proud of.

SAMPLE BOXED BOOK

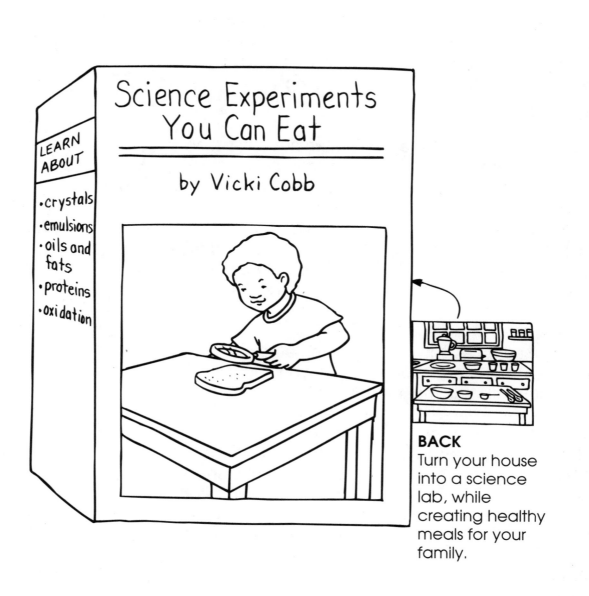

LEARN ABOUT

- crystals
- emulsions
- oils and fats
- proteins
- oxidation

Science Experiments You Can Eat

by Vicki Cobb

BACK
Turn your house into a science lab, while creating healthy meals for your family.

By the Same Author

After reading a good book, experienced readers will often return to the library and look for other titles by the same author. Usually, this is a good method for finding books worth reading.

Directions:

1. Choose an author who has written several fiction or nonfiction books on the same general subject. Some well-known examples are listed in the box below. Your librarian might help you find others.
2. Read at least two books by the author.
3. Write an article that tells about the author and about the books that you read. The article should explain how the books are alike and how they are different.

Follow-up:

Do the same activity with an actor, a painter, or any other creative person. For example, you might write about a musician who has made several albums that you like.

The BFG Dahl

Danny the Champion of the World Dahl

Charlie and the Chocolate Factory Dahl

James and the Giant Peach Dahl

FANTASTIC MR. FOX Dahl

George's Marvelous Medicine Dahl

The Twits Dahl

The Wonderful Story of Henry Sugar Dahl

The Enormous Crocodile Dahl

Nonfiction writers	Subjects
Franklyn Branley:	space science
Vicki Cobb:	science, experiments, health
Russell Freedman:	biographies and history
Gail Gibbons:	science and machines
David Macauley:	buildings
Pat McKissack:	minorities, culture, civil rights
Laurence Pringle:	ecology
Harvey Weiss:	machines, do-it-yourself

Fiction writers	Subjects
Judy Blume:	everyday life
Susan Cooper:	fantasy
Roald Dahl:	strange characters
Walter Farley:	horses
John Fitzgerald:	rural family life
Madeleine L'Engle:	science fiction
Mary Norton:	fantasy
Seymour Simon:	mystery/adventure

SAMPLE AUTHOR ARTICLE

Funny Fred Gwynne

Fred Gwynne was a TV and movie actor who was interested in the way we use words. He wrote several books about everyday phrases that can be confusing.

For example, in *The King Who Rained*, a little girl is puzzled by the word "reigned," which sounds exactly like "rained" but means something very different. "Reigned" means "was in power." Words that sound alike are called homonyms.

Gwynne also has fun with words that are used in unusual ways. For example, having "a frog in your throat" doesn't mean there's a live green thing in there. It means you have a raspy feeling. This kind of phrase is called "a figure of speech."

Gwynne uses pictures to get readers to see how the sound of language can fool us. For example, when the girl's mother says she's a little "hoarse," Gwynne draws her as a tiny "horse."

Gwynne's first word play book was so popular that he wrote others, including *A Chocolate Moose for Dinner* and *A Little Pigeon Toad*. Some of the jokes are a little hard to understand. For example, you need to know that there's a chocolate dessert called a "mousse." But lots of the humor is easy to get. For example, when the girl's dad talks about being in a "car pool," Gwynne shows cars swimming in a regular pool.

Anybody who likes to read and write, and who is a little bit silly, will enjoy reading Fred Gwynne's series of word books.

Ha-Ha
Ha-Ha Ha-Ha
Ha-Ha Ha-Ha
Ha-Ha Ha-Ha
Ha-Ha
Ha-Ha
Ha-Ha Ha-Ha
Ha-Ha
Ha-Ha
Ha-Ha
Ha-Ha
Ha-Ha Ha-Ha
Ha-Ha Ha-Ha
Ha-Ha Ha-Ha
Ha-Ha
Ha-Ha

Character and Reader

Good readers often compare themselves to the characters in the books they read.

Directions:
1. Choose a character from a book you have read. You might pick the hero, the villain, or someone else.
2. Draw a Venn diagram by overlapping two circles. Label one circle with your name and the other with the character's name.
3. Write facts that are true only for you in your circle. Write facts that are true only for the character in the character's circle. Write facts that are true for both of you in the overlapping area. Think about things such as: physical details (hair color, height, etc.); friends; family; hobbies; skills; places visited; problems; and so on.

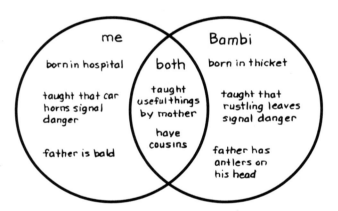

me — born in hospital; taught that car horns signal danger; father is bald

both — taught useful things by mother; have cousins

Bambi — born in thicket; taught that rustling leaves signal danger; father has antlers on his head

4. Pretend that you and the character are going to introduce each other to a group of strangers. Write a skit that tells what you have in common, and how you are different. Be sure to include the name of the book.
5. Find a friend who will take the part of the character. Then present your skit to your class.

Follow-up:
Do the same activity, but write about two characters within a book, for example, the hero and the villain. Or compare two characters from two different books.

SAMPLE INTRODUCTIONS

Get to Know Red Riding Hood and Goldilocks

Red Riding Hood: Hi. I'm Red Riding Hood from the book *Little Red Riding Hood*.

Goldilocks: And I'm *Goldilocks from Goldilocks and the Three Bears*.

Red Riding Hood: We're going to tell you a little about ourselves.

Goldilocks: I'll start by telling you how we're alike. We're both girls, that's obvious. And we're known for a color. Everyone knows that I have blonde hair and that Red Riding Hood has a red hooded cloak. We also both have animal problems. Mine are with three bears, hers with one wolf. Also, we both get into trouble while visiting someone else's house.

Red Riding Hood: We're different in many ways. Goldilocks is more curious than I am and that's what got her into trouble. She entered the bears' house just because she wanted to see what was inside. I entered my grandma's house because I was bringing her some goodies. In the bears' house, Goldilocks falls asleep. But I had to be wide awake to deal with the wolf.

Goldilocks: But maybe the most important fact is true for both of us. We both escape with our lives.

Character Fan Club

There have been fan clubs for movie stars and pop singers. Why not start clubs for fictional characters?

Directions:
1. Find a group of readers to start a character fan club.
2. Choose the character to honor. It might be a person, such as Charlie from *Charlie and the Chocolate Factory.* Or a realistic animal, like Black Beauty. It could even be an imaginary being, such as Charlotte from *Charlotte's Web.*
3. Plan the fan club. Activities might include:
   - designing a symbol (a picture) that stands for the club; this symbol might appear on t-shirts, stationery, book jackets, and so on
   - writing rules for club members
   - writing a club song (maybe using an old tune)
   - picking a special day to honor the character (for example, an important day in the story, or the birthday of the author who created the character)
   - putting up displays about the character in the library or other public places
   - writing up new stories featuring the character

Follow-up:
If the author is still alive, send him or her news about the fan club, or write letters to the characters and send them to the author.

SAMPLE FAN CLUB MATERIALS

The Big Bad Wolf Fan Club

The Big Bad Wolf Club Song (to the tune of "Twinkle, Twinkle, Little Star")

Big Bad Wolf
We like you so,
Especially when
You huff and blow.

It's OK
To chase a pig,
Whether it is
Small or big.

Big Bad Wolf
You're fun to know.
Take a deep breath
And let it go.

The Big Bad Wolf Club Rules

1. Brush your teeth carefully, especially your canine teeth.
2. Practice huffing and puffing at least once a week.
3. On your birthday be sure to blow out all the candles in one blow.
4. Never climb down chimneys.

Characters' Panel

In a panel discussion a small group of people share their ideas about a subject. Usually, a panel involves real people. But with a little imagination, it's possible to create a make-believe panel of characters from a book.

Directions:

1. Read a book that has at least two characters.

2. Think about the big lesson or idea in the book. Then sum it up in a sentence or two. For example, a reader might decide that the main lesson in *Pinocchio* is "Tell the truth."

3. Write a script for an imaginary panel discussion held by two or more characters in your book. One character should start off by naming the book and its author. During the discussion, characters can:

- talk to each other
- ask each other questions
- talk directly to the audience
- show objects that relate to the book, for example, pictures or maps

Whatever is said should be based on material found in the book. By the end of the discussion, at least one character should talk about the book's most important lesson.

Follow-up:

Find one or more partners to help you put on your script as a panel discussion. The actors might wear costumes.

SAMPLE PANEL DISCUSSION

You Don't Have to Be a Scaredy-Cat

Boy: Hi. We're the two main characters in *There's a Nightmare in My Closet* by Mercer Mayer. I'm the boy.

Nightmare: And I'm the Nightmare.

Boy: The book's title might make you think it's a scary story.

Nightmare: But it isn't. It's about learning to be brave.

Boy: At the beginning of the story, I always made sure the closet door was closed. I thought that would keep the Nightmare from bothering me.

Nightmare: But you can't lock up a bad dream. A dream is just a thought in your head. In a way, when you have a bad dream you really are scaring yourself.

Boy: That's right. The only way to get un-scared is to face whatever you are afraid of. Instead of hiding under the covers, I sat and waited for the Nightmare.

Nightmare: I was just as afraid of you as you were of me.

Boy: That's what the book is all about. Things are really less scary when you don't run away from them.

Nightmare: Instead of scaring each other, we decided to be friends.

Boy: Of course, there are always other scary things to think about.

Nightmare: The author shows that by having another Nightmare come out of the closet on the last page.

Concentration

Concentration is a card game in which players try to make pairs by remembering where certain cards are placed. This game can be used to introduce readers to nonfiction books.

Directions:
1. Choose a nonfiction book.
2. As you read it, list about 10 interesting facts on scratch paper.
3. Using short sentences, write each fact on a note card. Then, make an exact copy of each card so that every fact is written on two different cards. On the front of each card, write the title of the book and the author's name.
4. Find two people to play a game of Concentration with your cards.
5. Shuffle the cards and lay them fact-side down in rows.
6. The first player turns up any two cards. If there's a match, the person gets those two cards and picks two more cards. If there isn't a match, the cards are turned fact-side down again, and the second player gets to pick.
7. After all the matches have been made, the winner is the person who has the most cards.

Follow-up:
Make a deck of Concentration cards based on a subject that you know about firsthand.

The first moon mission lasted eight days.

SAMPLE CONCENTRATION CARDS

These cards are based on the book *Apollo and the Moon Landing* by Gregory Vogt.

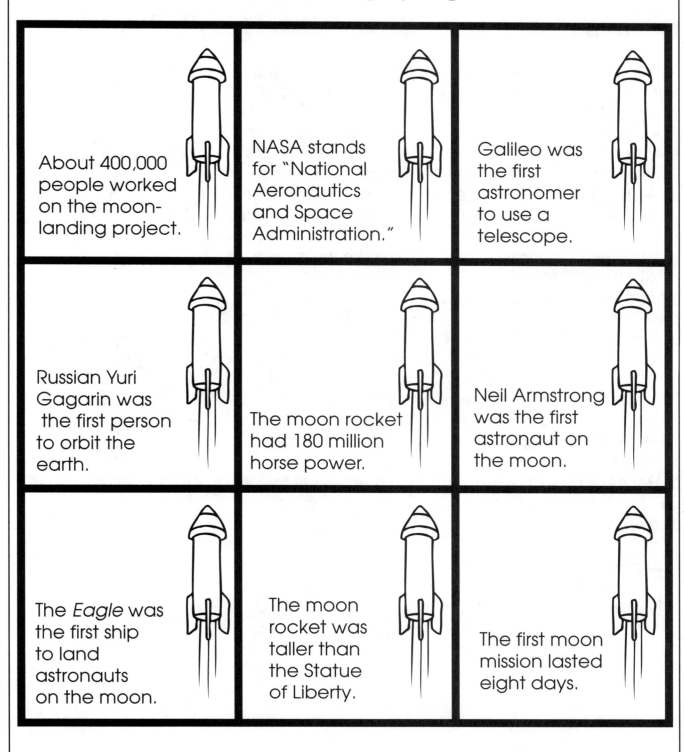

About 400,000 people worked on the moon-landing project.

NASA stands for "National Aeronautics and Space Administration."

Galileo was the first astronomer to use a telescope.

Russian Yuri Gagarin was the first person to orbit the earth.

The moon rocket had 180 million horse power.

Neil Armstrong was the first astronaut on the moon.

The *Eagle* was the first ship to land astronauts on the moon.

The moon rocket was taller than the Statue of Liberty.

The first moon mission lasted eight days.

Cooperative Book Chat

Every story is different from every other story. Yet two different stories will be alike in some ways.

Directions:
1. Find a partner.
2. Together, choose two similar storybooks or novels. For example, both books could be about outer space or they both could be about animals.
3. Each partner will read one of the books and fill out the Story Chart.
4. Together, use the two charts to plan a "compare-and-contrast" oral presentation. During the presentation, you will explain how the stories are alike and different. One of you might first list the similarities. Then the other will list the differences. Or you could take turns, with one of you comparing the characters, then the other comparing the settings, and so on. For example, in describing the characters in *Stevie* and *The Tenth Good Thing About Barney*, one partner might explain:

> The main characters in *Stevie* are people, two boys and the boys' parents. In *The Tenth Good Thing About Barney* there are also people characters—a boy, a girl, and the boy's parents. But the most important character is an animal—a dead cat.

5. Rehearse your presentation, and then give it to a live audience or do it on videotape. You might want to use posters to list the similarities and differences.

Follow-up:
Use the story chart to compare a story you've written with a story by a famous writer.

STORY CHART

What kinds of characters are there?
( ) humans   ( ) robots
( ) animals that act like humans   ( ) creatures from other planets
( ) animals that act like animals   ( ) ghosts or supernatural creatures

( ) others (list): _____

Where does the story take place?
( ) city   ( ) seashore
( ) desert   ( ) suburb
( ) forest   ( ) swamp
( ) outer space   ( ) underwater

( ) other places (list them): _____

When does the story take place?
( ) long ago   ( ) in the future
( ) in the present   ( ) can't tell

How long does the story last?
( ) a day or less   ( ) many years
( ) a few days or a few weeks   ( ) many centuries
( ) a few months to about a year   ( ) can't tell

What is the mood?
( ) funny ( ) gloomy ( ) serious ( ) other: _____

What important actions happen?
( ) chase   ( ) journey
( ) escape   ( ) race
( ) fight   ( ) search

( ) other (describe it): _____

What kind of ending is there?
( ) happy ( ) sad ( ) mixed

©1994 Monday Morning Books, Inc.

Dear Reader

Some characters are so interesting, it might be nice to have them as pen pals. But what kind of letters would they write?

Directions:
1. Choose a character from a book you have read. The character might be the hero, the villain, or someone else.
2. Pretend that the character wants to be your pen pal. Write a letter telling the character about yourself. Include a few questions that the character could answer.
3. Respond to your letter from the character's point of view. Before you write, reread your first letter, pretending to be the character who got it. This will give you ideas for the character's letter. You might write about things that happened in the book.
4. Continue the exchange a few times.
5. Bind the letters as a book of letters between a character and a reader. On the cover of this collection, include the title and the author of the book on which you based the letters.

Follow-up:
Imagine that two characters from two different books want to become pen pals. Try writing a series of letters between them. You might choose two characters who are alike in some way, for example, two kids who live in big cities. Or you could choose two very different characters, for example, The Big Bad Wolf and Snow White.

Hint: You might do this activity with a partner. Each of you would write letters from one of the characters.

SAMPLE PEN PAL EXCHANGE

Two Friendly Letters Based on *The Stupids Step Out* by Harry Allard

September 1

Dear Stanley Q. Stupid,
   I enjoyed reading about you and your stupid family. Sometimes the people in my family do dumb things, but next to you guys, we look like geniuses.
   There are three people in my family—my mom, my dad, and me. I'm a student. My favorite subject is science. Out of school, I like to go biking with my friends, and I'm learning to play the bassoon.
   I wonder how you feel about being so stupid. I mean, does it bother you if anyone asks why you named your dog "Kitty"? Do people laugh at you when you order things like "mashed potato sundae"?
   Please write back, if you know how to write.
                                    Your friend,

                                    A. Reader

September 43

Dear A. Reader,
   Thanks very much for writing to me. I hated your letter so much that I'm going to frame it and keep it forever.
   You asked how I feel about being stupid. The answer is yes. We call our dog "Kitty" because we didn't think she'd like being called "Fish" or "Bird" or "Worm."
   You made fun of our eating mashed potato sundaes. Have you ever tried one? They're yummy!
   I have to go now, to get ready for nothing this afternoon.
                                    Your pen pal,

                                    Stanley Q. Stupid

Diorama

A diorama is a three-dimensional display of a real or imaginary place. You can build a diorama to show a place described in a book you have read.

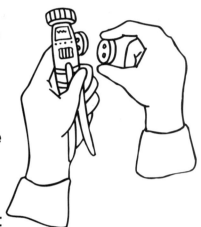

Directions:
1. Choose an important place from your book. For example, in a book about space travel, the place might be the inside of a rocket ship or a crater on the moon.
2. Sketch the place.
3. Gather materials needed to make the diorama. Diorama makers often use easy-to-find materials such as:
- bars of soap
- bottle caps
- clay
- cloth scraps
- clothespins
- corks
- empty thread spools
- shoelaces
- thumbtacks
- toothpicks
- watercolor paints
- yarn

For a backdrop, use a shoe box or a cardboard box.
4. Include a card or piece of paper that gives the title of the book, the author's name, and information about the place. Be sure to include your name, so that people will know who made the diorama.

Follow-up:
Create a diorama about a place from your own life.

SAMPLE DIORAMA

The Golden Spike ceremony described in
All Aboard! by Mary Elting

This book gives the history of American railroads
starting in the 1830s. One chapter describes how
workers from the East and from the West met at
Promontory, Utah. To celebrate the first trans-
continental railroad, the final spike was made
of gold.

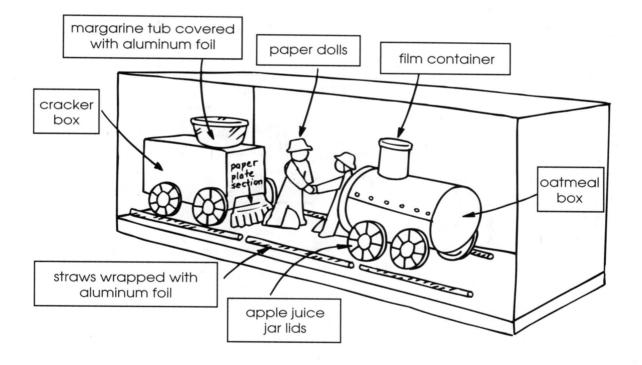

margarine tub covered with aluminum foil

paper dolls

film container

cracker box

oatmeal box

straws wrapped with aluminum foil

apple juice jar lids

paper plate section

Doing Dewey

Librarians sort nonfiction books into ten groups. Each group is numbered. For example, the "500s" group contains science books. Books about sports, games, and so on are in the 700s group. This way of keeping similar books together is called the "Dewey Decimal System."

Directions:
1. Go on a scavenger hunt through the nonfiction section of a library. From each of the ten main Dewey Decimal groups, choose one book that you might like to read.
2. Write the name of that book and its complete number in the Dewey Decimal Book Hunt Form. For example, Harvey Weiss' *Submarines and Other Underwater Craft* is numbered 623.825 W429s. The "W429s" part refers to the author's last name.
3. Circle the number of the group that includes the subject that you're most interested in. For example, if you're interested in doing magic tricks, you'll mark the 700s.

Follow-up:
Read one book from at least three of the groups.

DEWEY DECIMAL BOOK HUNT FORM

For each group, list a book that interests you. Include its complete Dewey Decimal number.

000-099   Reference and fact books
_____

100-199   Ideas and thinking
_____

200-299   Religion
_____

300-399   Social studies
_____

400-499   Languages
_____

500-599   Sciences
_____

600-699   Useful things
_____

700-799   Sports and games
_____

800-899   Literature
_____

900-999   History

Electronic Book Review

An electronic book presents a story or information on a computer or TV screen. In addition to printed words, it can include photographs, drawings, motion pictures, music, speech, and interactive activities. Of course, every electronic book isn't worth reading. As with "old-fashioned" books, readers will have to be choosy.

Directions:
1. Read an electronic book.
2. Take notes on the book using the Electronic Book Checklist.
3. Use the notes to write a review that describes the electronic book and that says whether other people might like it.

Follow-up:
Try to get your review published in your school or local newspaper.

ELECTRONIC BOOK CHECKLIST

Title of book: _____

Author: _____ Publisher: _____

Price: _____ Copyright year: _____

Type: ( ) fiction ( ) nonfiction ( ) reference
Purpose: ( ) entertainment ( ) education ( ) other _____
Format: ( ) computer disc ( ) CD-ROM ( ) laser disc
System it runs on: ( ) Macintosh ( ) IBM compatible ( ) other _____

Features: Quality (A = best to F = worst)
( ) animation   _____
( ) live action   _____
( ) photographs   _____
( ) drawings   _____
( ) maps   _____
( ) diagrams   _____
( ) speech   _____
( ) music   _____
( ) interaction   _____
( ) instruction manual   _____

Overall ease of use: ( ) very easy to use ( ) average ( ) hard to use

Describe this book's best features:

_____

_____

Describe what would make the book better:

_____

_____

Would you recommend this electronic book? _____

Extra! Extra!

The information inside a book can be turned into articles for an imaginary newspaper's front page. All it takes is a reader who wants to be a reporter.

Directions:
1. Choose about six events or topics from a book that you have read. In a book about whales, topics might include eating, swimming, and raising young whales.
2. Think up a newspaper name that refers to the book. For example, if your book is about volcanoes, the paper might be called *The Lava News*.
3. Decide how big your paper will be. For a realistic look, think about using a poster-size sheet.
4. Pick the most important topic or event. Draft an article about it using information from the book. Newspaper articles usually answer five questions in the first paragraph: who, what, why, where, and how. Give the article an interesting title.
5. Write shorter articles about the other topics.
6. After revising your articles, print or type them in columns for the final version of your paper. Use drawings or photographs to illustrate one or two of the articles.
7. Post your front page for others to read and enjoy.

Follow-up:
Write a newspaper front page about events in your life.

THE PINOCCHIO NEWS

Puppet Comes Alive

Inside a Shark

The History of Puppets

The Lives of Crickets

How the Nose Works

Fascinating Facts

What makes a book interesting? For many writers, the secret is to include lots of surprising details.

Directions:

1. Choose a nonfiction book on a subject that interests you.
2. As you read the book, list facts that you didn't know before and that you think are interesting. (A fact is a statement that can be proven through observation, for example, by weighing, or by studying documents.)
3. Make a poster about the book by listing some of the most surprising facts. Name the book and its author in the title of the poster. Add a short introduction that tells what the book is about.
4. Include one or a few pictures or diagrams to help explain what the book is about.
5. If you like, add a final line that urges readers to learn more from the book that inspired your poster.

Follow-up:

Do the same activity with a fiction book. Instead of facts, list amazing happenings. For example, in *Hansel and Gretel*, the list might include:

- The witch lives in a house made out of candy.
- Food turns into stones in the witch's stomach.

SAMPLE AMAZING FACTS POSTER

FACTS ABOUT CHRISTOPHER COLUMBUS

Christopher Columbus: Admiral of the Ocean Sea
by Jim Haskins

Everyone has heard of Christopher Columbus. But there are many surprising facts about this famous sailor. Here are some examples.

Fact 1. Columbus' real name was Cristoforo Colombo.

Fact 2. In Columbus' time, the word Indies meant China and Japan as well as India.

Fact 3. Columbus never set foot on land that today is the U.S.A.

Fact 4. In the 1980s, scientists used a computer to figure out where Columbus first landed. They believe it was Samana Key in the Bahamas.

Fact 5. On his first voyage to the New World, Columbus' ship, the Santa Maria, sank.

Read *Christopher Columbus: Admiral of the Ocean Sea* and you'll learn many other facts!

Film or Book?

Many movies are based on books. Audiences often enjoy comparing the book and film versions of the same story and deciding which is better.

Directions:
1. Choose a book that has been made into a movie or a television show.
2. Read the book and view the film. (It doesn't matter which you do first.)
3. Think about how the book and the film are alike and how they are different. You might organize your thoughts using a Venn diagram.
4. Write an article that compares the book and the film. You might point out things that were left out of the movie version or that were added to it. Tell which you like better—the book or the movie—and explain why. Or, if you like them the same, tell why that's so.

Follow-up:
Choose a movie or TV show that you like, and write it as a story. When you're done, decide which you like better: the film or your written version.

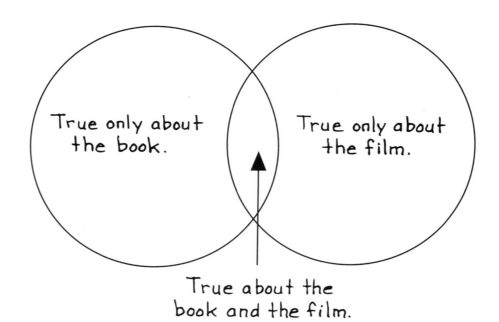

BOOKS MADE INTO FILMS

Most of these titles are available on videotape and/or laser disc.

Alice's Adventures in Wonderland
Around the World in 80 Days
Bambi
Beauty and the Beast
Black Beauty
The Black Stallion
The Call of the Wild
Charlie and the Chocolate Factory
Charlotte's Web
A Christmas Carol
Cinderella
Dr. Dolittle
The Grinch Who Stole Christmas
Huckleberry Finn
The Jungle Book
The Lady and the Tramp
Lassie
The Lion, the Witch and the Wardrobe
Mary Poppins
Mrs. Frisbee and the Rats of NIMH
One Hundred and One Dalmatians
Peter Pan
The Phantom Tollbooth
Pinocchio
The Red Pony
The Rescuers
Sarah Plain and Tall
The Secret Garden
Sleeping Beauty
To Kill a Mockingbird
Twenty Thousand Leagues Under the Sea
The War of the Worlds
The Wizard of Oz
The Yearling

Good Guy Award

Almost every book has at least one character who "does the right thing." This kind of character is a model everyone can learn from.

Directions:
1. After reading a book, choose a character whom you admire.
2. List one or several actions that made you like the character. Examples include doing a brave deed or mastering a difficult skill.
3. Think up the title of an honorary award that the character should win. For example, the third pig in *The Three Little Pigs* might win an award called "The Smart Builder Award."
4. Create a certificate that honors the character. Fill in the following information:
  • name of the award
  • name of the character who wins the award
  • name of the book and its author
  • what the book is about
  • why the character deserves the honor
5. Post the certificate in a place where readers are likely to see it, for example, in the library.

Follow-up:
Create a certificate honoring a real person you know and admire. It could be a friend, relative, neighbor, teacher, teammate, or anyone else in your life.

CHARACTER AWARD FORM

_____
(name of award)

This award is for _____,
(name of character)

a character in _____,
(name of book)

written by _____.
(name of author)

The book is about _____

_____

_____

_____

_____

The character deserves this award because _____

_____

_____

_____

_____

_____

_____

_____

Gossip Column

Gossip comes from the word "godparent." Long ago, gossip meant news about family and friends. Today, gossip includes talk about famous people. Although most people say that gossiping isn't nice, gossip columns are popular in newspapers, in magazines, and on television.

Directions:
1. Make a list of the most important characters in a book that you have read.
2. Next to each character's name, write a few interesting facts.
3. Now, imagine that you are a newspaper gossip writer (columnist). Write a column that tells the news about your characters. Each piece of news is called an "item." A gossip column is usually written in short sentences.
 4. Give your column a name that relates to the title of the book. For example, a column about "Goldilocks and the Three Bears" might be called "Bear Bits."
5. Publish your column in a class or school newspaper.

Follow-up:
 Write a gossip column about famous people in history. Or write a gossip column about objects treated as people, for example, "The Inside Information About a Cell."

SAMPLE GOSSIP COLUMN

Jack and the Beanstalk Talk

We've always known that Jack isn't the smartest guy in the world. But now we have more proof. We heard that he sold the family cow for a handful of "magic" beans. Smart thinking, Jack! Eyewitnesses say that a strange plant grew overnight near Jack's cottage. Those on the scene claim that the weed, which they call a beanstalk, is over 100 feet (30 meters) tall. Some people even say that it reaches the clouds. We'll believe that when we see some giant beans.

Speaking of giants, Jack, who disappeared for a day last week, told his friends that he actually had traveled to the castle of the giant who had killed Jack's father many years ago. According to Jack, the giant said things like "Fe fi fo fum, I smell the blood of an Englishman." That's a nice story, Jack. Do you really think anyone will believe that a giant makes rhymes?

People who live in Jack's neighborhood support Jack's story. They say that this poetic giant chased Jack down the beanstalk and almost caught him. Jack saved himself by cutting down the plant with an axe. We'll need to see some photographs or a videotape before we believe this one.

Guided Fantasy

When sharing an experience, storytellers will sometimes ask their listeners to close their eyes so they can imagine what it was like to be there. The same method works when sharing a scene in a book.

Directions:

1. Choose a dramatic scene from a book you have read. It should be something that one of the main characters experienced.

2. List details from the scene. Use words that relate to the five senses: seeing, hearing, smelling, touching, and tasting. For example:

   a noisy machine
   hot, sticky tar
   smelly garbage

3. In your own words, write a description of the scene. Start by naming the book and its author. Then ask listeners to close their eyes and imagine that they are a character in the book. Use the pronoun *you* to put listeners in the character's place. Try to make your description exciting by including many details.

4. End the description with a sentence that brings your listeners back home. Let them know when it's OK to open their eyes.

5. If you like, have the listeners draw pictures of what they saw during the guided fantasy.

Follow-up:

Take listeners on a guided fantasy of an experience that you had, or of an experience from science or history, for example, what an astronaut might have felt when walking on the moon. You might even give listeners the experience of being a white blood cell fighting germs inside the human body.

SAMPLE GUIDED FANTASY

You're on a Sinking Ship with the Black Stallion

Walter Farley's novel *The Black Stallion* is a thrilling horse story. In Chapter 2, "The Storm," the human hero, Alex, is on a ship when a storm hits.

Close your eyes and imagine that you're out at sea. You're sleeping in a cabin when a crash of thunder wakes you up. The ship is rolling back and forth with such violence that you're thrown out of your bed and onto the floor. Through a porthole, you see lightning cutting through the darkness.

You dress and rush to the deck. Other passengers are running toward the lifeboats. A huge wave carries a sailor overboard. People are screaming. The boat shakes.

You remember that the black stallion is in his stall. If the boat goes down, he'll drown. You decide to set him free. You hurry to where the horse is, and open the door.

The giant horse races by you and leaps overboard. As he jumps, he knocks you backward. You fall into the ocean.

When you come to the surface, you see the boat. There's an explosion. The ship begins to sink. Waves crush into you. There's no way you can stay afloat in this storm. You know you are going to drown.

Then you see the horse, swimming close by. A rope trails from his halter. It's your only hope. You reach. You grab it. You hold on. Now you find yourself being dragged through the water.

What will happen next? Read the book for yourself. But to do that, you'll have to open your eyes.

©1994 Monday Morning Books, Inc.

How to Do It

Readers often admire characters for their skills, for example, being able to fly a plane or build a house or ride a wild horse. Some of these skills can be learned by anyone willing to study and practice.

Directions:

1. List the most important skills of your book's hero. For example, the character might know how to sew, water ski, juggle, cook, solve crimes, or paint pictures.

2. Choose the skill that you think is the most unusual or the one that you'd like to be able to do yourself.

3. Write a set of directions that explains how to do the skill. Do the writing from the point of view of the character, for example,

    "How I Get Ready for a Ball"
        by Cinderella

4. If the book doesn't give you enough information, do research by reading about the skill in another book or by talking to someone who knows how to do it. If necessary, add pictures to explain how the skill is done.

5. In the introduction to the directions, give the title and the author of the book.

Follow-up:

Choose a skill you have, for example, flying kites or making pancakes. Write a story in which a character uses that skill.

The Girl Who Loves to Paint

SAMPLE DIRECTIONS

How to Hatch an Egg by Horton

My name is Horton and I'm an elephant. You may be surprised that an elephant can write, but I'm a special elephant. I'm from Dr. Seuss' book, *Horton Hatches the Egg*.

In the book, Mayzie the bird wants to go off and have fun, so she talks me into sitting on her egg. That's not an easy job for an elephant. I weigh a lot, and I could easily break an egg by sitting on it. However, I was very careful with Mayzie's egg, and I was able to hatch it. Here's how you can do it if you ever are asked to hatch an egg.

1. Before you sit on the egg, get some warm clothes and a raincoat or umbrella. You'll be spending lots of time outside. Different kinds of bird eggs take different amounts of time to hatch. Usually, the smaller the bird, the quicker its egg hatches. A pigeon egg hatches in about 18 days. A goose egg takes about a month.
2. Gather food and beverages.
3. Bring along a few books or cassettes. Sitting on an egg can get boring after a while.
4. When you are about to sit on the egg, move very slowly and don't let all your weight land on the egg. Eggshells are very delicate. You just want to barely touch the egg. The idea is to keep it nice and warm.
5. When it's about time for the egg to hatch, listen closely for the chick's beak pecking away at the shell. You don't have to help it. But it is a good idea for you to get off the egg to make room for it.

I hope this information will be useful to you if you ever have to hatch an egg. I also hope that you'll want to read about my adventure.

Index a Book

An index is an alphabetical list of topics often found near the end of a nonfiction book. Each item in the list is followed by one or more page numbers. These numbers tell readers where to find the topic. Fiction books rarely have indexes. But making an index for a story is a good way to learn how indexes work.

Directions:
1. Choose a storybook. Make sure it has page numbers.
2. As you read the book, list each important word or topic. For example, in the story of *Rumpelstiltskin*, topics include straw, a spinning wheel, and gold.
3. Next to each topic, list the page where you found it. If a topic appears on several pages, list each page number. However, if a word appears on almost every page, then you don't need to include it in your index. You want to list topics that readers need help finding.
4. When you reach the end of the book, put the topics into alphabetical order. Add a title that tells what book the index is for.

Follow-up:
Imagine that you are going to write a nonfiction book about a day or a week in your life. Brainstorm the topics that you might cover, for example: homework, chores, favorite TV shows, and so on. List these topics in order as if they were the index for your book.

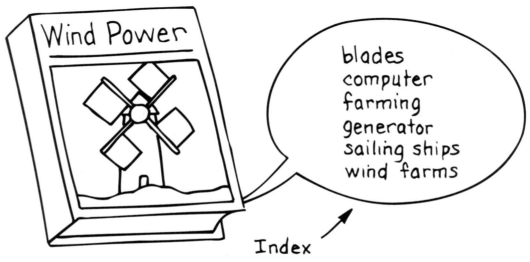

SAMPLE INDEX

Index for *The Stupids Step Out*
by Harry Allard

bannister riding, 8, 9
bath, 10, 11
bed, 30, 31
bedtime, 28
car ride, 17
cat, 12, 13
closet, 20, 21
Grandfather, 16, 18, 20
Grandmother, 16, 20
hat, 12
keyhole, 20
mashed potato sundae, 24, 26
meowing cat, 12
mirror, 23
parking the car, 22
restaurant, 25
sleeping clothes, 28
staring, 22
stockings, 14, 15
tub, 10
walking on hands, 27

Interview a Character

An interview is a talk between two people. One person, called the interviewer, asks questions about the other person's life or skills. The second person, called the interviewee, answers the questions. With imagination, it's possible to interview a character from a story.

Directions:
1. Choose a character from a book you have read.
2. Write a list of questions to ask the character about his or her adventures.
3. Write an introduction to the interview. It should include the title of the book and the name of the author.
4. Begin interviewing the character. Write the questions and answers in the form of a play. Put your name in front of each question, or use the word "interviewer." Put the character's name in front of each answer.
5. If you think up new questions during the interview, use them.
6. Try to end the interview with an interesting question and answer.
7. Add a title to the finished interview. The title might include the name of the person you interviewed.
8. Find a partner and perform the interview in front of an audience.

Follow-up:
Interview someone you know. After you polish the words, give the person a copy of the interview.

SAMPLE CHARACTER INTERVIEW

Talking to Sally, Heroine of Dr. Seuss' *The Cat in the Hat*

Sally and her brother are a couple of kids. One day, during a rainstorm, a very strange character visited them.

Interviewer: How did you know something was about to happen?

Sally: We heard a bump.

Interviewer: What was it?

Sally: The Cat in the Hat. He came right into our house.

Interviewer: What did he do?

Sally: He started showing us tricks. He juggled the goldfish bowl and frightened our fish, who said that the cat shouldn't be there.

Interviewer: Did the cat leave?

Sally: Not right away. First, he made a big mess. Two of his friends, Thing One and Thing Two, almost destroyed our house. Then the cat went away.

Interviewer: It sounds exciting.

Sally: At first it was. But then I started worrying that our mom would be very angry at us. But just before she came home, the Cat in the Hat came back with a machine and picked everything up. He left the house just as neat as it was when he started playing.

Interviewer: Would you like to play with him again some day?

Sally: Yes, now that I know that he cleans up after himself.

Job Application

In many books, characters show off their skills. For example, in *Little Red Riding Hood* the wolf uses his acting talent when he pretends to be Grandma. Maybe the wolf should have looked for a job in a theater.

Directions:
1. In a book you've read, find a character who has one or more skills. The skills can be real, for example, knowing how to bake a cake. Or they can be make-believe, for example, knowing how to become invisible.
2. Think up a job that the character might be able to do. Use your imagination. For example, the wolf in *The Three Little Pigs* might use his huffing-and-puffing skill to test how well houses are made.
3. Fill out the Job Application Form as if you were the character.

Follow-up:
List your own skills, and think about a job in which you might use one or more of them. Then fill out the Job Application Form for yourself.

WEAVER WANTED

JOB APPLICATION FORM

Fill in only the facts that you know. Do not make up answers.

Name: _____
          last   first   middle initial

Age: _____ Birthplace: _____

Address: _____

Name of book (if you live in a book): _____

Job you would like to have: _____

Education: _____

Skills: _____

_____

Describe something you have done that shows you can do the job. (This is called your "experience.")

_____

_____

_____

List two people who know you and will say what kind of worker you are. (These are called your "references.") Tell who each person is, for example, your cousin or your teacher.

_____

_____

Jump into the Action

It's fun to read an exciting book. But it can be even more fun to take part in the action.

Directions:
1. Choose a book with action that interests you, for example, riding horses or spying.
2. Pick a favorite scene. Or if it's a short book, use the whole book.
3. Write a new version of the scene or the book by including yourself as a character. You can talk to the other characters, help them, interfere, or do anything that fits the story. The results can be silly or serious.
4. In the introduction to your version, include the title of the book and its author's name.

Follow-up:
Do the same activity, but this time write a scene or story that puts you into a favorite movie or TV show.

SAMPLE JUMP-IN STORY

Max, Me, and the Wild Things

Max is a little kid who I met in *Where the Wild Things Are*, a book by Maurice Sendak.

Max upset his mom, so she sent him to bed without supper. Then, sort of by magic, a forest grew in his room. I know that sounds strange, but I saw it with my own eyes.

At the edge of the forest was the ocean. Max came to the shore and found a sailboat there with me in it. I was in the boat because it belongs to me.

"I'm Max," said Max. "Can I go for a ride in your boat?"

"Sure," I said. So off we went. It seemed like a long, long ride. Max thought it was a year, but it was much less. Anyway, we finally reached an island filled with Wild Things. They are scary-looking monsters, but they aren't as mean as they look.

They roared and jumped around, but Max wasn't afraid. He's a tough little kid. Of course, with me by his side, he didn't have much to worry about. I'm about five feet tall and weigh over 100 pounds. It would take something really wild to frighten me.

After a while, the Wild Things quieted down. They wanted to make friends with Max. They even called him their king. He liked that a lot. Pretty soon, we were having a great time, jumping around, yelling at the moon, and doing gymnastic tricks on tree branches. It was really fun.

But then Max got homesick. He asked me if I'd sail him back to his bedroom. I said, "Of course." And I did it. When we got there, he found that his mom had put out his dinner for him.

I told Max, "You have a really nice mom."

He didn't say anything, because his mouth was full of food. But he nodded. Then I got into my boat and sailed away, back to the island of those Wild Things. Maybe they'll make me king.

Letter to a Reading Pal

After reading a good book, it's nice to tell someone else about it. This is called "word of mouth" advertising, and it's what makes a book become popular.

Directions:
1. Choose a fiction or nonfiction book that you really enjoyed reading.
2. Brainstorm a list of people who might also enjoy this book. Hint: Think about the book's subject. For example, if the book is about flying kites, who do you know who already flies kites or who might be interested in a new outdoor hobby?
3. Write a letter telling about the book and why the person might like to read it. Be sure to include the book's exact title and the name of the author. You might also ask that person to recommend a book to you.

Follow-up:
Write a book recommendation letter to your school or local newspaper. This way, dozens or even hundreds of people will learn about your opinion.

SAMPLE READING PAL LETTER

January 8

Dear Mark,

Thanks for sending me the photographs of your baby pet mice. They look cute. Are you having fun watching them grow up? Maybe you'll become a mouse scientist some day.

I couldn't tell the mice apart. Can you? I read that a mother mouse can recognize each one of her babies. Maybe she does it by smell.

I was thinking about your mice this week because I was reading *Mrs. Frisbee and the Rats of NIMH*. It's by Robert O'Brien. Have you read it?

The story is about Mrs. Frisbee, a field mouse who meets up with a group of super-smart mice who were created by scientists. Maybe if you read the book, you'll learn how to teach your mice to solve difficult problems. But even if you can't do that, I think you'll really enjoy the book.

Write me again about how the mice are doing. Also, let me know if you have read any good books lately.

Your friend,

Nellie

Letter to the Editor

Most newspapers have a letters column. In it, the paper's readers can share their ideas about the news. They also can offer their solutions to all sorts of problems.

Directions:
1. Choose a fiction or nonfiction book with a character who has a problem that could be solved through a law or through efforts by ordinary people.
2. Think about how the problem might be solved.
3. Pretend that you are that character and write a letter to an imaginary newspaper. Your letter should begin by telling who you are. (Use details from the book.) Then the letter should describe the problem and what should be done about it.
4. Give your letter a title and add an introduction that mentions the book and its author.

Follow-up:
Write a real letter to the editor of your school or town newspaper. In the letter, describe a problem and give your solution to it.

SAMPLE LETTER TO THE EDITOR

Stop Those Monkeys

This letter might have been written by the hero of the book *Caps for Sale* by Esphyr Slobodkina.

To the Editor:

I am a peddler. I sell caps. You probably have seen me around town. I wear the caps I sell on my head. There are brown caps, white caps, gray caps, and red caps. They make a very tall stack, which I am able to balance.

I don't bother anybody. I just go here and there, selling caps to people who want to keep the sun out of their eyes or their heads warm. I do a real service to the community.

But I am angry about something. The other day no one needed a cap. Sometimes that happens. So, I went for a walk in the country and took a nap under a tree.

When I woke up, all of my caps were missing except for my own checked cap. I looked everywhere for the caps. And where do you think they were? On the heads of a group of monkeys up in the tree.

It took me all afternoon to get those caps back. And it happened only by accident. When I angrily threw my cap down on the ground, all the monkeys did the same thing.

I lost a lot of selling time because of this problem. I think it's terrible that people let their monkeys run free without supervision. There should be a law that says a monkey must be on a leash when outside.

I hope everyone who reads this will write to City Hall and support my plan.

Thanks for your help.

Sincerely,

A. Peddler

Meet the Author

It's interesting to learn about the people who create the books we like. It can be even more interesting to become these people for a few minutes.

Directions:
1. Choose an author whose writing you enjoy.
2. Gather information about the author. Your research might cover the following areas:
   - family background
   - education
   - books written
   - awards

Sources for this information include:
   - the author's notes in books written by the author
   - library reference books such as *Something About the Author* (Gale Research)
   - the author's publisher

3. Use the facts you collect to write an imaginary interview of the author. Include an introduction that lets readers know that this is a made-up interview.
4. Find a partner and use your interview as a script for a presentation. One of you will play the interviewer; the other will play the author. Perform the script "live" in front of an audience, or record it on audiotape or videotape.

Follow-up:
Do the same activity, but this time write an interview with a famous person from history.

SAMPLE MEET-THE-AUTHOR SCRIPT

Leslie Tryon's Very Creative Life

Leslie Tryon is one of the country's best picture-book author/illustrators.

Interviewer: What made you want to create picture books?

Leslie: I've always been interested in the arts. Before I published my first picture book, I drew illustrations for the *Los Angeles Times* and I worked on books for teachers.

Interviewer: What was your first picture book?

Leslie: *Albert's Alphabet.* It's the story of a duck who works at a school. He's given the job of making an outdoor alphabet. When he runs out of materials, he uses his imagination and building skills to make letters out of all sorts of things.

Interviewer: Albert is really smart.

Leslie: He is very resourceful.

Interviewer: Albert also appears in *Albert's Play*. This tells how the children at Pleasant Valley School put on *The Owl and the Pussy-cat*. Were you ever in a play?

Leslie: Well, I've been a dancer, and I've written plays for children. I love theater and enjoy the teamwork needed to put on a show.

Interviewer: Is Pleasant Valley a real place?

Leslie: I made it up. But in some ways it's like the places I've lived. I've lived in San Fernando Valley, Simi Valley, and now Carmel Valley. I guess I like valleys.

Interviewer: Will Albert appear in all of your books?

Leslie: Not all of them. But he'll definitely appear in many of them. He's a character I like very much.

Mural of a Scene

Good writers know how to use words to help readers "see" things in their imaginations. It can be exciting to turn one of these word pictures into a mural. This project can be done by one person or by a small group.

Directions:
1. After reading a fiction or nonfiction book, choose an important or dramatic scene.
2. Make a small practice sketch of this scene. If you don't know how something looks—for example, a helicopter—it's OK to do research before you draw. Find a picture of the thing in a book and use that picture as a model for your drawing.
3. Use your small sketch as a guide to draw a mural of the scene on poster board or butcher paper. Add ink and color to give the picture a finished look.
4. Write a caption that tells what the scene is all about. Include the title of the book and the author. After editing the caption, copy it onto clean paper and attach the paper to the mural.
5. Post your mural in a library, classroom, or hallway where it might make people interested in reading the book.

Follow-up:
Make a mural that shows all the important scenes from a book. This might be done as a group project.

The Death of Aslan in
The Lion, the Witch, and the Wardrobe
by C.S. Lewis

Museum Display

Enter an American Plains Indian home, based on *The Tipi*, a book by Charlotte Yue.

Books often include descriptions of interesting objects. A three-dimensional display of these things can entertain and teach. It can also invite people to learn more by stepping inside the pages of the book.

Directions:

1. Choose one or a few objects that play an important role in a book that you have read.
2. Figure out how to represent the object or objects in a display. For example, if your book is about sea life, you might use a real seashell or you might make a lifestyle clay model.
   - If an object is huge—for example, a jetliner—you will need to find or make a small model.
   - If the object is tiny—for example, a blood cell—you might make a large model.
3. Write a paragraph about each item in the display. After you edit each paragraph, copy it in large-size type on a clean sheet of paper or on a note card.
4. Write an introduction to the entire display. Include the title of the book and its author, and tell how the object or objects fit into the book.
5. Set up the display in an area where people can see it but not bump into it. If there are valuable items, you might put the display in a locked glass case.

Follow-up:

Make a display about something you know firsthand. It could be about a hobby, for example, model trains. Or it could be about an experience you had, for example, visiting Africa.

SAMPLE MUSEUM DISPLAY

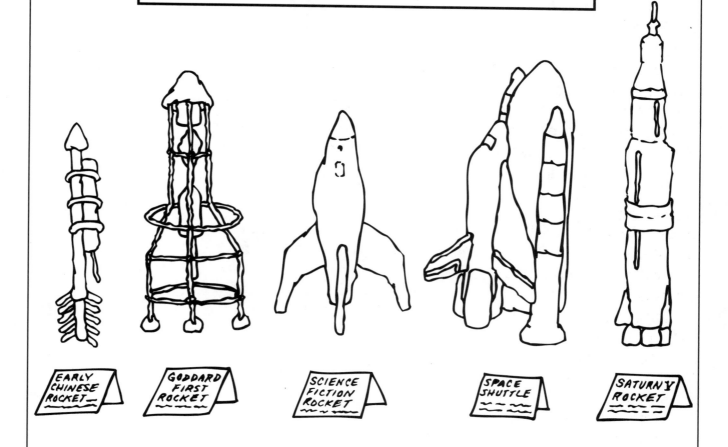

A History of Rockets
based on the book
Space, Stars, Planets and Spacecraft
by Sue Becklake

EARLY CHINESE ROCKET

GODDARD FIRST ROCKET

SCIENCE FICTION ROCKET

SPACE SHUTTLE

SATURN V ROCKET

Quilt a Story

Successful story writers create word pictures that are so clear readers can turn them into real pictures.

Directions:
1. Choose a book that has at least a dozen interesting scenes.
2. Do a pencil sketch of each scene on a separate piece of paper. Then go over the lines in ink. Erase the pencil marks. Add color by using crayons, markers, or watercolor paint.
3. Tape the scenes together to make a paper quilt.
4. Use one block to give the title of the book and the author's name.
5. Near the bottom of the quilt, attach a note card or piece of paper that gives a short summary of the book.
6. Hang the quilt up in your classroom or in the library.

Follow-up:
Create a quilt that tells about your life. It could include pictures about your home, your family, your friends, your hobbies, and your plans.

SAMPLE STORY QUILT

Story Quilt for *Charlotte's Web*

Charlotte's Web

by E. B. White

Quiz and Teach

Quizzes are usually given to find out what people have learned. But quizzes can also be used to interest people in a subject they haven't yet studied.

Directions:
1. Choose a nonfiction book on a subject that you want to know more about.
2. As you read the book, list interesting facts.
3. When you've finished the book, write a question for each fact. There are three main kinds of questions:
- true or false, for example:
    The sun is a star. True or false?
- fill in the blank, for example:
    The sun is a _____.
- multiple choice, for example:
    The sun is a) a planet, b) a star, c) a comet.

In your quiz, you can use just one kind of question or you can use two or three kinds.
4. Write an answer for each question. If possible, include an explanation or a short piece of interesting information in the answer.
5. Put together the finished quiz. Include a title and an introduction that gives the title and the author of the book the quiz is based on. You might print the answers upside down or on a different page.

Follow-up:
Share the quiz in your school or town newspaper, or post it on a bulletin board.

SAMPLE QUIZ

How Much Do You Know About Insects?

Insects can be a bother. But they are also one of the most interesting kinds of animals. Here is a quiz based on *Insect Zoo* by Susan Meyers.

1. Insects were on the earth before dinosaurs.　　True　　False

2. Most of the animals on earth are insects.　　True　　False

3. Insect zoos can be found in many countries.　　True　　False

4. Spiders are a kind of insect.　　True　　False

5. Centipedes have 100 legs.　　True　　False

6. Insects and birds are the only animals that fly.　　True　　False

7. Some insects survive by eating live animals.　　True　　False

8. Some insects are born live, like human beings.　　True　　False

9. The female giant water bug lays her eggs on the back of the male.　　True　　False

10. An insect's skeleton is the outside of its body.　　True　　False

Answers
1. True. Insect scientists (entomologists) believe insects have existed for nearly 400 million years, 150 million years before dinosaurs.
2. True. About 80 percent of living creatures are insects.
3. True. England, Germany, and Japan are examples.
4. False. Insects have six legs. Spiders have eight.
5. False. Some centipedes have more than 200 legs.
6. False. There is one more type of flying animal—bats.
7. True. These are called predators.
8. False. All insects are born from eggs.
9. True. The male carries the eggs on his back for two or three weeks.
10. True. This is why insects have "hard" bodies.

Radio Commercial

Radio commercials play for only a minute or less. Every second counts. That's why making a successful commercial takes a lot of creativity. Hear for yourself.

Directions:
1. Choose a book you enjoyed reading.
2. List what you liked about the book.
3. Decide which type of radio commercial you want to make. There are two main types:
   - **Announcer only:** An announcer talks directly to the audience and tells what's good about the product.
   - **Dialogue:** Two or more actors talk to each other as if in a play. During the talk, they get across the idea that the product is worth buying.
4. Write a script. A 60-second commercial uses between 100 and 200 words. The script should explain why people might like the book. It also should mention the book's name at least three times so that listeners can remember it.
5. Test the script by reading it aloud and timing it. You may need to add or cut words.
6. Cast the script. This means finding one or more people to speak the lines.
7. Rehearse the script so that all actors can smoothly read their lines. Make sure there aren't gaps (silences) when one person stops talking and another starts.
8. Record the commercial.

Follow-up:
Create a tape-recorded radio play based on the book or on an original story. This kind of play usually is between 15 and 30 minutes long. It may include sound effects, such as doors slamming, meant to add realism.

SAMPLE RADIO COMMERCIAL

Announcer-Only Commercial
for *Stellaluna*

ANNOUNCER: Let's talk about bats. I don't mean baseball bats. I mean those wonderful flying creatures that sleep during the day and zip around at night. Some people are afraid of bats. But if you get to know these flying mammals, you'll see that they aren't scary at all.

Stellaluna by Janell Cannon is a storybook about a baby fruit bat who gets separated from her mother. Stellaluna falls into a bird's nest and grows up acting like a bird. She becomes part of a family with three young birds, Pip, Flitter, and Flap. Later, after she finds her mother, Stellaluna teaches the birds about the good points of being a bat.

Stellaluna is not a science book. The animal characters talk and have human feelings. The story is more about friendship than about "Chiroptera," which is the scientific name for bats.

However, *Stellaluna* does include excellent drawings of bats. It also has two pages of facts about the different kinds of bats. For some readers, *Stellaluna* may be a first step in learning about these flying mammals. And there is a lot to learn. For example, some bats have wingspans of six feet! You won't find a baseball bat as big as that.

Report Card for a Book

Every book has a job to do. Some books teach. Others entertain. Like human workers, books can be graded on how well they carry out their tasks.

Directions:
1. Choose any book that you have read. It can be one that you liked or one that you hated.
2. Grade the book using the Report Card for a Book form. Or create your own form.
3. Publish the report card in your school paper or by posting it on a bulletin board.

Follow-up:
Write and fill out a report card for a movie or TV show.

REPORT CARD FOR A BOOK

Title of the book: _____

Author of the book: _____

Type of book: ( ) fiction ( ) nonfiction

Subject matter (e.g., animals, a famous person, medicine, music, sports):

_____

Give each of the following items a grade from "5" (best) to "0" (worst). Skip items that do not apply to your book.

Was the topic interesting?   _____

How good was the art (drawings and/or photos)?   _____

Were the characters worth knowing?   _____

Was the writing clear?   _____

Overall grade: _____

Best thing about the book: _____

Worst thing about the book: _____

Advice that you would give the author: _____

_____

_____

_____

Review for a Newspaper

Many newspapers and magazines publish articles about new books. These articles are called "reviews" and they tell readers what's in the books. They also say whether or not the books are worth reading.

Directions:
1. Choose a book to review. Don't worry if it's good or not. You can write an interesting review about a bad book.
2. Before or while reading the book, write the following:
   • title of book
   • author of book
   • publisher of book
   • copyright date
   • type of book: fiction or nonfiction
   • number of pages
   • audience for the book

3. As you read the book, form an opinion about it. Is the book good, bad, or mixed?
4. Copy a few sentences from the book that show what it's like. For example, if you think the book is exciting, copy an exciting passage. If you think it is hard to read, copy a passage that you think is confusing.
5. When you're done reading the book, write a report that describes what's in the book and that gives your opinion about it. Include some or all of the information from your notes. If you know of a book on the same subject, you might compare the book you are reviewing with the other book. Hint: If the book tells a story, don't give away the ending.
6. Give your review a title that sums up your opinion about the book, for example, "An Exciting Dog Adventure."

Follow-up:
Send your review to the school or town newspaper. Later, you might write a movie review.

Have Fun with Math Tricks

Take one sheet of a newspaper. See if you can fold it over on itself ten times. You can't do it, can you? Don't feel bad. No one can do it, not even the strongest person in the world.

The reason is simple. Each time you fold the paper, you double its thickness. The first fold involves two sheets. The second four sheets. The third eight sheets. By the time you reach seven, it's 128 sheets.

This kind of doubling is a very important math process, and just one of the things you'll learn in *Math-a-Magic* by Laurence B. White and Ray Broekel (published by Whitman & Company, 1990). This 48-page book includes nearly two dozen tricks for magicians or for anyone who wants to entertain friends or family members. There are tricks that use coins, fingers, calculators, and even an imaginary piano.

You don't have to be a magician to do the tricks. The steps for each one are carefully described. The authors also explain the math idea behind the trick, so that you'll be learning a basic skill while becoming an entertainer.

Scene Flip Book

Most books contain one very dramatic action that readers remember even if they forget everything else about the book. It can be exciting to capture such an action in a "paper" movie.

Directions:
1. Choose an important action from a book. It should be an action that is simple to draw and that lasts only a few seconds, for example, a volcano exploding or someone diving off a cliff.
2. In pencil, draw the beginning of the action on the blank side of a note card. If the action includes a character, try using a stick figure.
3. Draw the same scene but change it a bit as if a second or less has passed.
4. Continue drawing cards until you have a stack of ten or more.
5. Hold the stack of cards at one end and flip them to see the action. If the action is too jumpy, try drawing more cards and putting them into the stack at the right place.
6. When the flip book works the way you want it to, go back over each card and ink in the drawings.
7. Make a title card that gives the name of the book and its author.

Follow-up:
Draw a flip book that dramatizes an action in your life. For example, if you play soccer, it could show you kicking a goal.

The boat is moving!

 Flip Book assembly:
Put repeating pictures in sequence to form a flip book. Staple pages along left edge.

SAMPLE SCENE FLIP BOOK

Flip Book for *The Three Little Pigs*

Sequel to a Story

A sequel is a story that continues an earlier story. It tells what happens to one or more of the characters. For example, *Cinderella* ends with Cinderella's marriage. A sequel might tell about Cinderella's life after she moves into the castle.

Directions:
1. Choose a book with an ending that could lead to new adventures. For example, maybe the main character has found a treasure.
2. Think of a new problem that the character might face. For example, maybe a villain will try to steal the treasure.
3. Outline the action for the story.
4. Give the story a title that tells readers your story is a sequel. You might mention characters from the first story. For example, a sequel to *Goldilocks and the Three Bears* could be called: *Goldilocks Makes Friends with Baby Bear*.
5. Write the sequel in a way that's like the old story. For example, if the old story was told in rhyme, make your story rhyme.
6. On the title page, under the title of your story, give the title of the first story and the author's name if you know it.

Follow-up:
Write an imaginative sequel to a real event in your life. For example, if you just learned how to dive off a diving board, you might write a story in which you learn how to sky dive.

SAMPLE SEQUEL

"Alexander's Terrible Day at the Amusement Park" based on *Alexander, and the terrible, horrible, no good, very bad day* by Judith Viorst

Our family was going to the amusement park. I love that place. But on the way, we had a flat tire. My parents weren't happy when they saw that I had let the air out of the spare tire while I was playing with it. My father said he hoped this wasn't the start of a terrible day.

When we got to the park, I ran to my favorite ride, "The Scary Coaster." It lasts only a minute, but it's really exciting. I guess everybody likes it because the line was about a mile long. While waiting, I chased a balloon that someone had let go, and I lost my place and had to go to the end of the line.

Then a thunderstorm blew in. The ride was closed for safety reasons. I said that it was terrible to keep us waiting. But the attendant said it would be even more terrible to be hit by lightning.

After the storm, some big kids took my favorite seat at the front of the coaster. Some even bigger kids took the last car. I had to sit in the middle. I hate the middle.

The ride up the coaster's first hill was so exciting that I forgot what kind of day I was having. But then something broke and the coaster came to a stop way up high.

Talk about terrible, horrible, no good, very bad days at the park. But when I finally got down, my mother told me that I was lucky. I got to have an hour-long coaster ride. Mom always sees the good side of things that I think are no good at all.

Stories Can Teach

Fiction is any story that includes made-up parts, for example, animals that talk. But fiction often includes information about real people, places, and things. For example, a fictional story about a family that moves to Mars might give facts about rockets and outer space.

Directions:
1. Choose a book of fiction.
2. As you read the book, list facts that you find. For example, in *The Country Bunny and the Little Gold Shoes*, it is true that:
   - bunnies eat carrots
   - bunnies have paws
   - bunnies can run fast
   - many children receive baskets of Easter eggs
3. Make a poster that tells about a few facts in your book. You might include pictures that help explain the facts.

Follow-up:
Pick a subject that you know a lot about. Then write a short fictional story that includes facts about your subject. For example, if you know how to play the piano, you might make up a story about a mouse who learns to play the piano. Your story could include real facts about music.

SAMPLE STORY TEACHING POSTER

Weather and the Wonderful Wizard of Oz

Frank Baum's book about the land of Oz is mostly make-believe. In it are talking monkeys, a talking scarecrow, a man made out of tin, and a cowardly lion. Most of the story takes place in a dream. But some parts are true. For example, it's true that tin will rust if it gets wet.

One of the most interesting factual parts of the book is the description of the life on a Kansas farm about 100 years ago. The book tells how a tornado forms when winds come from the north, south, east, and west at the same moment. It also explains that Kansas houses had storm cellars to protect people from a terrible storm.

Storyboard

Many books have been made into movies. Examples include *Beauty and the Beast* and *The Phantom Tollbooth*. An important step in making a movie is creating a picture outline, which is called a storyboard.

Directions:
1. Pick a scene from the book you have. A scene is whatever happens in one place. For example, there might be a scene in a kitchen or in a cave.
2. List each important action in the scene.
3. Divide a piece of paper into four or six boxes.
4. In the first box, draw the first action. Use only enough details to make the action clear. Stick figures are usually good enough.
5. If you like, under each picture write a few words or a sentence that explains the action.
6. Test your story by showing it to someone and explaining it as you go along.

Follow-up:
Make a storyboard that shows a scene from your own life, for example, something that happened to you on the playground or on a trip.

SAMPLE STORYBOARD

Storyboard for
"Down the Rabbit Hole"
from *Alice's Adventures in Wonderland*
by Lewis Carroll

1.

Alice gets sleepy.

2.

3.

4.

5.

6.

Story Diary

Most stories contain a series of smaller stories, each of which takes place at a certain time. It's easy to imagine a character in the story keeping track of the events in a diary.

Directions:
1. Choose a character from a book that you have read.
2. List the important events in the character's life. You can do this from memory or by skimming the book.
3. Pretend that you are the character, and are keeping a diary. Describe each important event in a separate paragraph, called an "entry." Write the entries in your own words. If possible, tell how much time has passed since the last entry. Sometimes you may have to guess.
4. Give the diary a title. Tell what book the diary is based on, and include the author's name.

Follow-up:
Keep a diary of your own life for at least a week. You might be surprised at how many interesting things happen to you. You might find ideas that you can use in writing your own stories.

SAMPLE STORY DIARY

The Velveteen Rabbit's Diary, based on *The Velveteen Rabbit* by Margery Williams

Entry 1.
   It's Christmas. I was given to a little boy. After a while he didn't pay much attention to me.

Entry 2. Many days later.
   The other toys think they're better than me because they have moving parts. I'm just stuffed with sawdust. The only nice toy is a wise, old horse. I asked him what is "REAL." He said it's what happens to you when a child loves you for a long time. I'd like to be real.

Entry 3. Months later.
   It's spring. The boy often plays with me outside. I've become very dirty. But I don't mind. The boy loves me and says that I'm REAL. That makes me very happy.

Entry 4. Months later.
   It's summer. While I was outside, I saw some strange rabbits. They jumped around, but I couldn't see what made them go. They asked me to play with them. I didn't tell them that I have no spring inside. But they saw that I don't have any hind legs. They laughed at me.

Entry 5. Weeks later.
   The boy has been sick for a long time. Now he's better and tomorrow will visit the seaside. I can't wait to go with him.

Entry 6. The next day.
   The boy's doctor said that all the boy's old toys have to be burned to get rid of the germs. I was thrown out with all of them. I felt so sad I began to cry. Then, where a tear had fallen, a wonderful flower grew. When it opened, a beautiful fairy spoke to me and turned me into a real rabbit. I was so happy I leaped into the air.

Story Sounds

The world is filled with all sorts of sounds, from the soothing rhythm of a clothes dryer to the scary screech of automobile brakes. Creative writers often weave sounds into their stories.

Directions:
1. List as many sounds as you can that relate to your book. Examples might include thunder, the beat of galloping horses, the roar of a rocket, or the wail of a police siren.
2. Choose one of these sounds. It might be the most interesting, the most important, or the most surprising.
3. Write an oral report that tells about the scene in which the sound happens. Explain how that scene is important to the entire book. Be sure to mention the title of the book and its author in your presentation.
4. Practice making the sound. You can use your voice, your hands, or an object to make the sound.
5. Rehearse your report by reading the words and making the sound at the right moment.
6. Present your sound report to the class.

Follow-up:
Write a story or report about one or a few important sounds in your life.

SAMPLE SOUND PRESENTATION

The Roar in *Where the Wild Things Are* by Maurice Sendak

(Make a loud roaring sound)

Do you like that sound? I do. It's the sound a little boy named Max heard when he got to the land of the Wild Things. The Wild Things are strange-looking creatures who live far across the water. To get there, you have to go by boat. That's what Max did after he was sent to his room without his supper. He was being punished for scaring his family's dog and doing other wild things.

After Max went to his room, the place began to change. Trees grew. Then the ocean appeared. Max found a little sailboat and used it to sail away from home.

When he got to where the Wild Things are, he wasn't afraid of the scary-looking creatures. He knew how to tame them with a stare. The Wild Things made him their king.

But after a while, Max got homesick. He decided to sail back to his bedroom even though the Wild Things wanted him to stay. That's when they really began to roar. They made wild noises. But Max had to go home.

At home, he found his dinner waiting for him. He probably made a lot of noise eating it. But it wouldn't be as much noise as the roaring of Wild Things. (Make roaring sound again.)

Telephone Call

Characters are usually trapped in their own stories. But what if they could phone up characters in other stories? Listening to them talk might be very interesting.

Directions:
1. With a partner, choose two books to read. You'll read one, and your partner will read the other.
2. Choose a character from your book, and have your partner choose a character from his or her book.
3. Together, imagine a phone conversation between the two characters. The conversation should explain what happened in both books.
4. Write a script of the conversation. Include the names of the two characters early in the call, so that people in the audience will know who's talking to whom.

Follow-up:
Turn your script into a play starring the two characters.

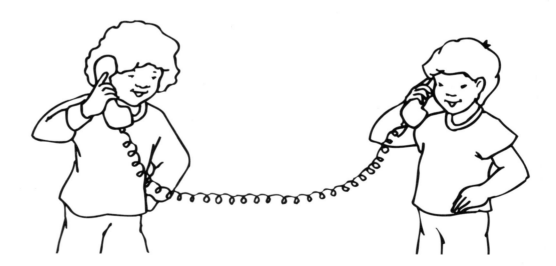

SAMPLE TELEPHONE TALK

A Call Between the Giant and Rumpelstiltskin

Sound: (Telephone rings.)

Giant: Hello? This is the Giant. Who is it?

Rumpelstiltskin: It's me. Rumpelstiltskin.

Giant: How are you?

Rumpelstiltskin: Terrible.

Giant: You sound far off.

Rumpelstiltskin: I am. I stomped my foot so hard that I made a hole in the ground and fell through it.

Giant: Why were you stomping?

Rumpelstiltskin: This girl guessed my name, so I couldn't keep her child.

Giant: That's awful. But what happened to me is worse.

Rumpelstiltskin: Oh, yeah?

Giant: This kid named Jack climbed a beanstalk up to my castle and stole my goose.

Rumpelstiltskin: What's the big deal about a goose?

Giant: It lays golden eggs.

Rumpelstiltskin: Why don't you call the police?

Giant: I can't do that. I stole the goose in the first place.

Rumpelstiltskin: I think my story is sadder. I broke my foot!

Giant: Sorry to hear that. But I've got to find a new goose. Bye.

Thrill Ride

Many amusement parks around the country offer rides based on stories, such as *Peter Pan* and *Twenty Thousand Leagues Under the Sea*. While building such a ride can cost millions of dollars, imagining one is free.

Directions:
1. While reading a book, look for exciting actions. These include: chases, races, visits to unusual places, trips taken in strange vehicles, amazing discoveries, and meetings with weird creatures.
2. Choose one of these actions and plan an amusement park ride that would put people into the middle of things. Your plan should include the following:
   - name of ride
   - list of things seen while on the ride
   - kind of vehicle—roller coaster, boat, electric car, horse-drawn cart, whatever
3. Draw your ride. You could make one big picture that shows the entire ride. Or you could draw a series of pictures. At the top or bottom of your picture, tell what book the ride is based on.

Follow-up:
Write a short description of what it would be like to go on your ride. Or write a one-minute radio commercial advertising the ride.

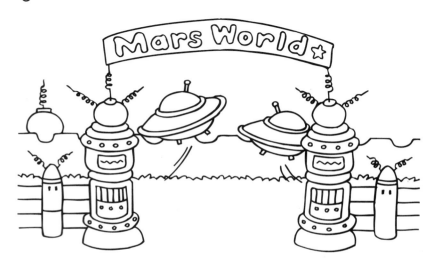

Time Line

Every story takes place over time. The time can be an hour, a day, a week, or longer. Good readers learn how to pay attention to the passing of time in the stories they read. One way to practice this skill is to make a time line.

Directions:

1. While reading a book, list each important moment. Tell how long it comes after the previous event. For example, the third event might be "the next day" or "many months later."
2. On a separate sheet of paper, draw a picture for each important event in the story. Label each picture with a word or phrase that tells when it happens.
3. Hang all of the moments from a string or post them on a bulletin board.
4. Begin the time line with a page that gives the title of the book, the name of the author, and a brief summary of the book's plot.

Follow-up:

Make a time line that shows the events that take place during a day or a week in your life.

SAMPLE TIME LINE

Time Line for *The Island of the Skog*

Tour Guide Speech

At many famous places, such as Niagara Falls and Buckingham Palace, a guide points out interesting things for visitors to see. Usually, what the guide says has been written ahead of time. Writing that kind of speech can be a challenging task, even if the place exists only in the imagination.

Directions:
1. After reading your book, choose the most interesting place where action occurs.
2. List the main parts of that place. Each part should be mentioned in the story.
3. Write a speech that a character in the story might give if showing a reader around the place. Include the title of the book, the name of the character, and something about the subject.

Follow-up:
Create a tour guide speech for a real place, such as your school, your neighborhood, or your home.

SAMPLE TOUR GUIDE SPEECH

A Visit to Mr. McGregor's Garden

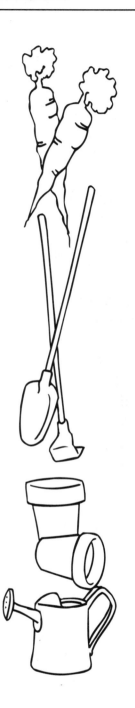

Hi. My name is Peter Rabbit. I'm a character in the book *The Tale of Peter Rabbit* by Beatrix Potter. Lots of exciting things happen to me in this book. Most of the action takes place in a garden owned by Mr. McGregor. Mr. McGregor doesn't like me. I guess it's because I try to take his carrots without his permission. But I don't think he'll mind if I show you around the place.

Let me begin here at his gate. People can easily open or close gates. But rabbits don't have hands to open the latch. We find it easier to dig right under the fence. Rabbits are excellent diggers thanks to our sharp claws.

Now let's go inside the garden. Here you see many delicious-looking vegetables. At least they're delicious to anyone who enjoys eating vegetables. We rabbits love carrots, peas, turnips, and all sorts of greens.

Mr. McGregor plants different kinds of vegetables. Over there, near the gate, you'll find corn, peas, and carrots. In the middle of the garden, there's alfalfa and broccoli.

If you look to the right side of the garden, you'll see a shed. That's where Mr. McGregor keeps his tools and flower pots. There are lots of good places to hide in the shed.

Now let's walk to the back of the garden. See that scary-looking creature? Don't worry. It's not alive. It's just a scarecrow. Maybe it does scare away the crows, but it doesn't bother me.

This is the end of our tour. I was going to take you to my family's home, which is located under a tree. But it's a secret place and I don't think I should tell you just where it is.

However, you can learn more about it when you read *The Tale of Peter Rabbit*.

Trade a Tale

Stories often remind us of happenings in our own lives. These memories can lead us to write new stories.

Directions:
1. After reading a book, list several of the story's most interesting scenes, such as an accident, a fight, or someone eating an unusual meal.
2. Think of an event in your life that is like one of the events in the book. For example, if the story tells about a character who got lost, maybe you'll remember a time when you got lost.
3. Write a letter to a character in the book, telling your story.

Follow-up:
If the author of the book is still alive, you might send your letter to him or her. You can mail the letter to the author in care of the book's publisher.

SAMPLE TRADE-A-TALE LETTER

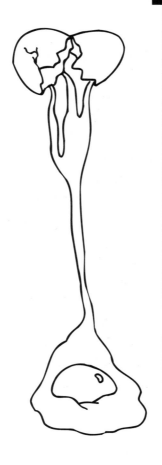

December 1

Dear Ramona,

I enjoyed reading about you in the book *Ramona Quimby, Age 8* by Beverly Cleary. You must have been embarrassed when your hard-boiled egg turned out to be real and broke all over you at lunch time! It's no fun to have raw egg on your face!

Your exciting story reminded me of something that happened to me when I was about four years old. I was going to nursery school. Every morning, around 10:30, we were supposed to take a nap. We'd all spread out mats on the floor. The teacher told us to close our eyes and lie still.

I don't know about the other kids, but I could never fall asleep. I'd toss and turn. Sometimes the teacher would be upset with me. Then I'd try harder to fall asleep, but the more I tried, the more awake I'd be.

One day, I opened my eyes and saw that the teacher had gone into the other room. All the other kids had their eyes closed. I got up and tiptoed to a door at the back of the room. I always wanted to know where it led. I opened the door and went out. I found myself on a little wooden porch behind the school. I let the door go and it closed. When I tried to open it, I found it was locked. I couldn't get back in.

I started crying, but that didn't help. Then I went down the steps from the porch, and I walked around the building until I came to the front of the school. I was afraid, but what could I do? I went in and found my teacher there. Was she surprised!

Nothing bad happened to me. But I was told never to do that again. And I didn't. However, I still wasn't able to fall asleep at nap time.

Sincerely yours,

A. Reader

Video Book Review Show

Two readers often have very different opinions of the same book. By sharing their thoughts, each of them may learn something new about the book. An audience who gets to listen to such a discussion can also learn a lot.

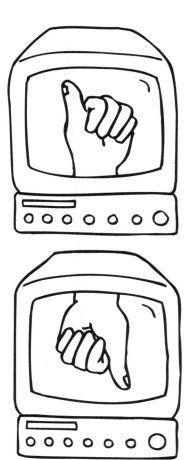

Directions:
1. Find a partner to appear on a television book review program with you.
2. Choose a book that you both will read and review. Each of you should take notes on the book. But do not discuss your feelings about the book before you go on the show.
3. Agree on a script for the show. This means deciding who will introduce the program, who will talk first, how long each person will talk, and who will have the last word. Here's a plan for a three-minute show:
   - Reviewer 1 greets the audience: 30 seconds
   - Reviewer 2 reviews the book: 60 seconds
   - Reviewer 1 discusses the book and agrees or disagrees with Reviewer 2: 60 seconds
   - Reviewer 2 sums up what both reviewers said and ends the show: 30 seconds
4. Decide what pictures to use, if any. If the book has pictures, you might wish to hold up one or two pages. In some cases, you might find or create art that relates to the subject. For example, you could use a globe in a review of a book about a voyage.
5. Rehearse what you're going to say about the book. You may find it helpful to write out the words even if you don't plan to read them.
6. Arrange for someone to video tape the presentation. Later, play the tape for classmates or other readers.

Follow-up:
Use the same format to review a film, a television show, or a cassette tape.

SAMPLE VIDEO SCRIPT

The Book Talk Show

Reviewer 1: Welcome to "Book Talk." This is the show where you can find out which books are worth reading, and which are not. Today, we're going to be discussing *Time to get out of the bath, Shirley* by John Burningham.

Reviewer 2: This is a picture book about Shirley, a girl who is taking a bath. Does that sound like the start of a boring story? Well, keep reading. When her mother isn't looking, Shirley slips down the drain, out of the house, and into a fantastic world of knights and castles and adventures. All the while, Shirley's mother is telling Shirley things to do, like pick up her clothes. It's very funny, and I strongly recommend the book to anyone who has ever been bored in the bathtub.

Reviewer 1: I agree with you that this is a wonderful book. The mother is very real. And that makes it even more funny, because what happens to Shirley is very unreal. Also, the pictures are beautiful. (Hold up a sample picture.)

Reviewer 2: So that's two thumbs up for *Time to get out of the bath, Shirley.* We're out of time now, but tune in next week when we'll be discussing *The Stinky Cheese* by Jon Scieszka.

Reviewer 1: Good-bye.

Who's Who

Most books are about people or about creatures that act like people, for example, talking animals or robots. Writing a short biography (life story) about each of a book's main characters is a good way to understand what a book is about.

Directions:
1. After reading a book, choose two or three characters you think are the most important.
2. Write a paragraph about each character. You might tell the following:
   • what the character looks like
   • what skills the character has
   • how the character talks and acts
   • how the character behaves (responsibly, wildly, etc.)
   • what kind of friends the character has
3. If you like, draw pictures of some or all of the characters.
4. Write an introduction that gives the title of the book, the name of the author, and a summary of the action.

Follow-up:
Write a short biography about someone in your life.

SAMPLE WHO'S WHO

The Stars of *The Cat in the Hat*
by Dr. Seuss

The Cat in the Hat tells the story of two bored children who are visited by a strange cat on a rainy day. The cat nearly gets the children into big trouble. But everything works out OK in the end.

The boy: He's about ten years old, has black hair, and a round face. He's a good problem solver and he can run quickly. He also isn't afraid to say what he's thinking.

The fish: He is a small, red creature who lives in a bowl and who knows how to talk. He also worries a lot. He doesn't see anything funny about what the cat does. He complains about every trick. But he is smart. He sees that the cat is going to make a mess of the house. He warns the children to stop the cat before it's too late.

The cat: He's a showoff. He wears a tall red and white cloth hat and loves to have fun. The cat has many talents. He can juggle, balance on a beach ball, and play wild games. He seems very silly at first, but he also knows that it's important to clean up after playing games. He uses a weird clean-up machine to straighten up the house before the children's mother returns.

Word Search

Words are keys that can unlock a book's main ideas. The following activity gets at those big ideas, while also providing practice in writing definitions.

Directions:
1. List five or more important words from your book. Choose character names, things, actions, or ideas. For example, in *The Wonderful Wizard of Oz*, important words include: Dorothy, Kansas, tornado, home, courage, and wizard.
2. Make a grid. Then write your words into the grid. Words can go across or down.
3. Write in other letters to disguise your words.
4. Give the grid a title that mentions your book and its author. Add an introduction that tells the reader how to use the grid.
5. On the page, list the words hidden in the grid. Or, for a greater challenge, give definitions of the words as clues to help searchers find them.
6. Make an answer key that shows where the words are hidden. You can use a highlighter pen or circle the words.

Follow-up:
Try the same activity with a current events article from a newspaper or magazine. Or use it with a story that you have written.

SAMPLE WORD SEARCH

Dinosaur Dig Word Search

See if you can find the following words in the letter grid. The words come from the book *Dinosaur Dig* by Kathryn Lasky and all of the words have to do with hunting for dinosaurs. The answer key is printed upside down. To learn what the words mean, read *Dinosaur Dig*.

awls
bone
dinosaur
dig
dirt
earth
fossil
fragile
plaster
resin

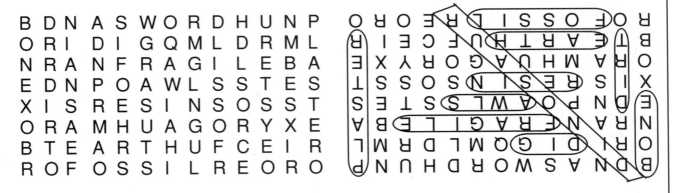

```
B D N A S W O R D H U N P
O R I D I G Q M L D R M L
N R A N F R A G I L E B A
E D N P O A W L S S T E S
X I S R E S I N S O S S T
O R A M H U A G O R Y X E
B T E A R T H U F C E I R
R O F O S S I L R E O R O
```

TEACHER TIPS FOR GROUP PROJECTS

Reading and writing don't have to be solitary activities. The following group activities can create a social environment that nurtures literacy.

Author of the Year: During the year, focus on an author. Students might:
- celebrate the author's birthday
- study the author's life
- read many of the author's books—solo and in groups
- create library or classroom displays of scenes from the author's books
- write to the author, if he or she is alive

Book Club Discussion Group: From time to time, have everyone read the same book. Then divide the class into small groups and have the members share their reactions to the book. You might provide students with a list of general discussion topics, such as:
- favorite part of the book
- least favorite part of the book
- question about the book
- personal experience relating to the book
- another book or film that relates to the book
- lesson learned from the book

To help students understand how such a discussion group works, you might arrange for a demonstration in front of the class. This model group might consist of a few students, or of adults (aides, parents, older students).

Book Week Celebration: Plan a variety of activities as part of National Library Week (April). These experiences might include:
- writing to the local newspaper about favorite books
- sponsoring a reading poster contest
- holding a homemade book fair
- involving parents in a week-long reading project in which the TV plays second fiddle to books
- holding an assembly featuring one or more local authors

Bulletin Board Brigade: Have students maintain a reading-oriented bulletin board in a hallway or in the library. Topics for the board might include:
- news about new books
- descriptions of under-used library resources
- biographies of favorite writers
- tips for doing library research
- news about prize-winning books

Character Sketches: While reading a book aloud, stop after a passage that describes a major character and have all the students draw their visions of the character. Post these picture biographies and discuss the similarities and differences.

Choral Readings: Have the whole class, or small groups, read aloud passages from all sorts of books. The reading can be in unison, or it can be done responsively, with two groups reading alternate paragraphs.

Class Reading Exchange: Pair up with a class in another school, the farther away the better. On a regular basis, say, once a month, exchange class-written letters telling about books read that month and reading-related projects, for example, putting on a play based on a book. Students might exchange videotaped book reviews.

Group Research Project: Choose a topic that contains many subtopics, for example, countries of the world. Have each student (or a small group) read and present a book that relates to the theme. Collaborative topics include:
- animals
- artists
- explorers
- heroes
- inventors
- jobs
- natural wonders
- planets
- sciences

Library Scavenger Hunts: Form students into small groups and have them scour the library in search of certain kinds of books. A sample scavenger hunt list might include the following categories:
- a book written by two authors
- a book in a series
- a book with color photographs
- a book written before the scavenger hunters were born
- a book that teaches a skill (e.g., juggling)
- a book with an index
- two books on the same subject

Predictions: Read aloud a chapter book. At the end of each chapter, have students, working alone or in small groups, write their prediction of what will happen in the next chapter. Students can share their predictions orally, or they can post them on a predictions bulletin board.

Reading Records: Have students constantly update a chart of special books they have read, for example:
- the book with the most pages
- the oldest book
- the book with the most chapters
- the biggest book (size of page)
- the smallest book (size of page)
- the book with the longest title

Sustained Oral Reading: In addition to a sustained silent reading program, which involves solo reading for a set number of minutes daily, devote a few minutes each day to oral reading. Divide the class into groups of about five students. For a minute, each student in a group reads aloud a passage from a book or magazine. Reading aloud with clarity and conviction is a key editing technique. It's also a skill that plays an important part in many jobs.

Writer in Residence Program: Arrange for a local writer to meet with your class on a regular basis, say, monthly or every other month. During these meetings, the guest writer might share news about a current project, give a lesson about writing, and listen to students read their work aloud.

TEACHER'S LIST OF BOOK GUIDES

The following resource books, available in many libraries, can help you locate good books in a variety of subject areas and at all reading levels.

A to Zoo: Subject Access to Children's Picture Books by Carolyn & John Lima (Bowker, updated regularly). Indexes scores of topics such as African-Americans, arts, dreams, and sports.

Adventuring with Books: A Booklist for Pre-K-Grade 6 by Dianne Monson (National Council of Teachers of English, 1985). Lists hundreds of books, with emphasis on fiction.

African-Asian Reading Guide for Children and Young Adults by Jeanette Hotchkiss (Scarecrow, 1976). Covers many regions and includes biographies, folklore, fiction, and nonfiction.

Best Books for Children Preschool through Grade 6 by John Gillespie & Corrine Naden (Bowker, updated regularly). Covers literature, arts, biography, history, science, society, geography, personal development, recreation, and curiosities.

The Best in Children's Books (series) by Zena Sutherland, Betsy Hearne, & Roger Sutton (U. of Chicago, 1991). Detailed reviews indexed by reading level, subject, and type of literature.

Black Authors & Illustrators of Children's Books: A Biographical Dictionary by Barbara Rollock (Garland, NY, 1992).

The Bookfinder: When Kids Need Books by Sharon Dreyer (American Guidance Service, updated often). Covers topics such as accidents, addiction, competition, and injustice.

Books by African-American Authors and Illustrators for Children and Young Adults by Helen Williams (American Library Association, Chicago, 1991). Very detailed index.

Books Kids Will Sit Still For: The Complete Read-Aloud Guide by Judy Freeman (Bowker, 1990). Covers fiction and nonfiction for grades K through 6, plus tips on storytelling, poetry, nonfiction, and "101 Ways to Celebrate Books."

Children's Books: Awards & Prizes by the Children's Book Council (updated frequently). Lists books chosen by adults and by children, from throughout the U.S. and abroad.

Choices: A Core Collection for Young Reluctant Readers by Carolyn Flemming & Donna Schatt (John Burke, 1983). Titles organized by grade level and interest. Topics range from Hank Aaron to "why" stories.

Eyeopeners! How to Choose and Use Children's Books About Real People, Places, and Things by Beverly Kobrin (Penguin, 1988). Probably the best resource for building a nonfiction reading program. In addition to reviewing 500 books, it offers 150 tips for book-based activities, plus a method for linking fact and fiction.

A Guide to Non-sexist Children's Books edited by Denise Wilms and Ilene Cooper (Academy Chicago Publishers, 1987). Topics covered include American Indian life, astronauts, athletes, careers, Latino life and culture, dance, farming, law, rodeo, slavery, war, and women in film.

A Hispanic Heritage by Isabel Schon (Scarecrow, 1991). Covers Argentina, Central America, Chile, Mexico, and other nations and regions. Subjects include well-known Hispanic people as well as politics, government, customs, music, and other topics.

Introducing Bookplots: A Book Talk Guide for Use with Readers Ages 8-12 by Diana Spirt (Bowker, 1988). Includes reviews, basic plot concepts, and strategies for book talks.

Literature for Science and Mathematics, Kindergarten Through Grade Twelve (California Department of Education, Box 271, Sacramento, CA 95812, 1991). Links specific titles to the math and science curriculum.

More Exciting, Funny, Scary, Short, Different, and Sad Books Kids Like About Animals, Science, Sports, Families, Songs, and Other Things by Frances Carroll and Mary Meacham (American Library Association, 1988). Features kid-style groupings, such as "I Want a Twisted Folktale," "Where Are the Dinosaur Books?", "Do You Have Any Books About Aliens?", "Do You Have Any Pop-up Books?"

The New Read-Aloud Handbook by Jim Trelease (Penguin, 1989). Covers do's and don'ts of reading aloud, and offers detailed write-ups of predictable books, wordless books, picture books, reference books, novels, and poetry.

The New York Times Parent's Guide to the Best Books for Children by Eden Lipson (Times Books, 1989). Not just for parents, it covers 1,000 titles, and cross-indexes them a dozen ways.

A Reference Guide to Historical Fiction for Children and Young Adults by Lynda Adamson (Greenwood Press, 1987). Covers prehistory, Roman Empire, Eastern empires, the crusades, and other periods.

Using Picture Storybooks to Teach Literary Devices: Recommended Books for Children and Adults by Susan Hall (Oryz Press, 1990). Lists specific titles for teaching simile, exaggeration, and other figures of speech.

STUDENT MEDIA TIPS

The following hints can help you create better projects.

Live Presentations: panels, speeches, skits, puppet shows, and so on
• Plan the presentation. If you're giving a speech, it's usually best to write out a script even if you don't plan to use it during the talk. It's very important to know exactly how you'll begin and exactly how you'll end.
• Keep the presentation short. Audiences get bored easily.
• Give attention to the setting and the materials you'll use (props). Make sure pictures or objects are big enough to be seen at the back of the room.
• Rehearse the presentation several times. Practice speaking in a clear voice. Try not to fidget or make distracting body motions. Ask a trial audience for suggestions.
• Walk onto the stage or speaking area with confidence. Get set before you start talking.
• If you're giving a speech, make eye contact with people in the audience. Even if you are reading the words, look up from the paper from time to time. If you're taking part in a panel, look at the people who are sharing the stage with you. If you're in a skit or play, ignore the audience and focus on your fellow actors.

Print Products: newspapers, magazines, books, posters, and so on

• Think about your audience and your purpose.

• Keep it short. You'll do better to leave readers wanting more than less.

• Focus on interesting facts. Don't tell readers what they already know.

• After you polish your words, read the draft aloud to yourself. If you hear rough spots, make changes. Then ask a trial reader to look over your draft and give you suggestions for improving it.

• Edit the final draft for spelling and punctuation.

• Give the project an interesting title. The title should let readers know something important about what you have written.

• Give the finished work eye appeal. Use large lettering for the title and think about adding a picture on the cover or front page.

• Don't crowd pages with type. Leave wide margins, in which you can place art.

Puppet Shows: puppets only, puppets and people, video puppet programs

• Be imaginative. Puppet shows can deal with any subject, from astronomy to zoos. Characters can take part in panels, teach lessons, and act in skits.

• Create puppets from items such as tin cans, shoe boxes, paper cutouts, toys, soap bars, spoons, and kitchen tools. (How about an eggbeater puppet who talks about nutrition?) A few details will do. For example, a piece of red cloth on a sock can make a Red Riding Hood puppet.

• Keep the script short. Limit the cast to a few characters and avoid long speeches. Use chases, dances, and other simple actions.

• Build a sturdy stage.

• Rehearse carefully. Because puppets are small, their actions seem speeded up. Practice moving them slowly. Have people in a trial audience tell you how the show looks and sounds.

Radio: tape-recorded speeches, skits, commercials, and so on

• Script the program. Remember, listeners can't see what's going on.
• Plan a real beginning and a real ending.
• Think about ways to use music and sound effects.
• Rehearse several times before recording.
• Record in a quiet room. Take care not to rustle the script.
• Place the microphone close to the mouths of the speakers.
• Label the finished cassette with the name of the show, the date, and the talent (the people who take part in the program).

Television: videotaped panels, skits, and so on
• Plan to keep the program short and simple.
• Script the program. Plan a strong beginning and a real ending.
• Hold the camera steady. If possible, put it on a tripod.
• Use backdrops when possible. For example, a news program might look more professional if there's a map behind the newscaster or a picture of your town.
• Don't crowd the stage. You'll do better with small casts.
• Give extra attention to sound. While most people think pictures are the most important part of a TV show, bad sound will quickly distract viewers.
• Rehearse the program several times before taping it.
• When talking to viewers, look directly into the camera. If the show is a panel discussion, panel members should usually look at each other, not at the camera.
• Label the recorded tape with the show's title, talent, length, and date.

©1994 Monday Morning Books, Inc.

STUDENT WRITING TIPS

Drafting

Don't expect a project to come out right when you begin to work on it. The first draft (also called the "rough draft") is a chance to put your ideas into words. Often, the order of ideas will be confused. Sentences may not make sense. But don't worry. The purpose of writing this draft is to help you get ready to polish your ideas.

This isn't the time to worry about neatness or spelling. If you're writing by hand, leave wide margins and skip every other line. This way, you'll be able to make changes without having to copy over everything.

Editing

After you finish the first draft, put your work aside for a time. Then read it slowly. Some writers read their work aloud. Make changes by crossing out words you don't need, by adding others, and by moving parts around. When you feel that the words make sense, you might read them aloud to someone, to see if the words are clear. Then check the spelling and the punctuation and make a clean copy of the work.

Length

Don't judge a project by how long it is. A very good one-page script is much better than a poor ten-page script. Professional writers know that a great deal of work must go into every page. For example, writing a one-minute radio commercial might take a day, a week, or longer.

Punctuation

If you're writing by hand, underline the title of a book or a movie that you are writing about, for example:

> In <u>The Black Stallion</u>, a boy named Alec Ramsay tames a wild horse.

If you're using a computer printer that can make italic type, then print a book title or a movie title in italic, a kind of slanting type:

> In *The Black Stallion*, a boy named Alec Ramsay tames a wild horse.

STUDENT SELF-EVALUATION FORM

Your name: _____   Date: _____

Title of project: _____

Type of project:
( ) art   ( ) radio program   ( ) TV show
( ) speech   ( ) written work   ( ) other _____

Strengths of this project (what's good about it):

_____

_____

Weaknesses of this project (how it could be better):

_____

_____

Interesting experiences you had while working on this project:

_____

_____

Skills you practiced while working on this project:

_____

_____

Advice for anyone else trying this kind of project:

_____

_____

Comments (use the back of this paper or another sheet):

INDEX